Networking with Novell NetWare

A LAN Manager's Handbook

Paul Christiansen
Steve King
Mark Munger

 WINDCREST®

Windcrest books are published by Windcrest Books, a division of TAB BOOKS Inc. The name "Windcrest" is a registered trademark of TAB BOOKS Inc.

Published by **Windcrest Books**
FIRST EDITION/FIRST PRINTING

Library of Congress Cataloging-in-Publication Data

Christiansen, Paul 1947-
    Networking with Novell NetWare: a LAN manager's handbook / by
  Paul Christiansen, Steve King, and Mark Munger.
      p.   cm.
   ISBN 0-8306-9283-5   ISBN 0-8306-3283-2 (pbk.)
   1. Local area networks (Computer networks)   2. NetWare (Computer operating
system) I. King, Steve. II. Munger, Mark. III. Title.
  TK5105.7.C48   1989
  004.6'8—dc20   89-28643
                                              CIP

TAB BOOKS Inc. offers software for sale. For information and a catalog, please contact TAB Software Department, Blue Ridge Summit, PA 17294-0850.

Questions regarding the content of this book should be addressed to:

Windcrest Books
Division of TAB BOOKS Inc.
Blue Ridge Summit, PA 17294-0850

Acquisitions Editor: Stephen Moore
Manuscript Editor: Pat Mulholland-McCarty
Production: Katherine Brown

Contents

_____PART II_____

Security and Accounting

PART III

Printing

---

8 Printer Installation and Capturing   *97*

_____PART IV_____

Electronic Mail and Productivity
Enhancement Software

_____PART V_____

Menuing Systems and Front-Ends

_____PART VI_____

Supplemental Software

_____PART VII_____

Other NetWares

Introduction

NETWORKS have become increasingly important in recent years. Their growth, to a large extent, has paralleled that of microcomputers in business. Historically, microcomputers entered mainstream businesses through the back door. Individuals and managers brought their PCs to work and began increasing individual productivity within their work sphere of influence. Slowly, PCs began to be recognized as important tools and slowly became integrated into the overall business computing strategy.

As PCs proliferated, there began to be more and more problems with distributing software, maintaining data, sharing files and coordinating workflow. It is in this environment that networks began to make their impact.

What is a network? Stated simply, a *network* is a means to allow for the sharing of system-wide resources among users. Typically these resources are programs, printers and data. Networks provide other capabilities as well, such as the ability for convenient E-Mail, group scheduling, workgroup management, gateways and bridges into other computer environments and hardware multitasking.

There are two major types of PC networks. The first is a *peer-to-peer network*. In this scheme, each user on the network has (potential) access to any other users resources. Thus user A can use user B's hard disk drive and printers, and user B can use user A's hard disk drive and printers. Peer-to-peer networks are relatively easy to implement and use, provided the number of users is small and the performance needs are relatively minimal. The second type of network is a *client-server based network*. In this design, one or more PCs are set up as a "file server" or "network server."

File-server based network systems are normally a lot more powerful and have increased capability compared to peer-to-peer network designs. The reason for this is simple. In a peer-to-peer system, the network exists as a guest, or task, on a DOS machine. All of the DOS limitations therefore apply, like volume sizes, file structures, lack of security, lack of multi-tasking design, etc. In a client-server based network design, the file server runs on software which is, in fact, an operating system. NetWare, by Novell, is a *network operating system*. Network operating systems take over the entire machine and typically use proprietary disk formatting schemes, file structures and file access methods. This is why advanced features like elevator seeking, read-after-write verification, disk mirroring and duplexing, security, system-wide accounting features, etc. can be implemented within the operating system.

In this book, *network* is used to mean a group of personal computers connected by means of network adapters (cards) and network cabling to one or more file servers. This is the Novell implementation of a client-server network operating system.

Some additional terms need to be defined. A personal computer attached to a network is normally referred to as a *workstation* and a connection to the network cable is referred to as a *node*. Thus a file server and five workstations would comprise a 6-node network.

SUMMARY

Novell today is the dominant player in microcomputer networking. They have succeeded in setting the standard for performance, system design and reliability. NetWare will likely remain a major player in this market for the foreseeable future.

PART I

Network Essentials

1

Networking Basics

A PC-based network consists of a *network interface card* (NIC) connected to a network cable that links the PCs and any file servers to form a network. Most file servers use the same type of NIC as a workstation. From the perspective of network cabling, no differences exist between a file server and a workstation. Some manufacturers do produce expensive, high performance NICs that you can use in a file server to increase the overall performance of the network, while you use less expensive, lower performance cards in workstations.

Networks can have a variety of configurations, called *topologies*. Three major topologies have been defined: star, linear bus, and ring.

A *star network* takes a file server as the center of the star, as you can see in Fig. 1-1. A cable from each workstation connects directly to a port on the file server at the center of the star. We know of no true star topologies being produced today. Of most note, several years ago Novell produced an S-Net server that had a true star configuration.

A second topology, *ring*, has a configuration that connects each workstation to cabling that forms a complete ring, as shown in Fig. 1-2. IBM's token ring network provides an example of a currently manufactured network that uses a ring topology.

The third topology, *linear bus*, uses a single cable laid out along the length of the network. Each workstation is either directly connected to the bus or is connected to it with a *drop cable*. Figure 1-3 illustrates a linear

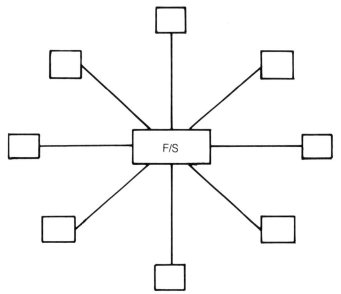

Fig. 1-1. Star topology.

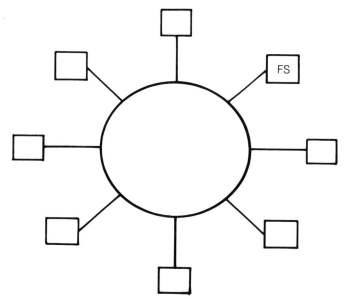

Fig. 1-2. Ring topology.

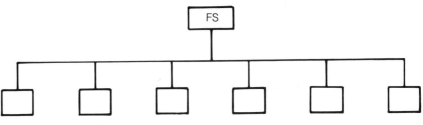

Fig. 1-3. Bus topology.

bus-type LAN topology. The most common linear bus implementation is Ethernet. However, other older and/or non-standard LANs, such as Vlan, G-Net and Omninet, also use a bus topology.

NETWORK STANDARDS

Today, the LAN world essentially has three major de facto standards, each roughly corresponding to one of the three topologies. Ethernet uses linear bus; Token Ring uses ring; ARCnet uses star—actually a string of stars.

ARCnet provides medium performance and low cost networking to many business environments. It also gives you an ideal LAN starting platform and is the entry level system we recommend.

Ethernet has an international standard that provides excellent performance and interconnectability for networks using dissimilar platforms and operating systems. Ethernet, a mature and well respected networking standard, has the largest installed base of network nodes in the world.

Token Ring, the new kid on the block, was developed by IBM as the centerpiece of its PC networking strategy. Token Ring has found a comfortable home in the Fortune 1000 arena where an IBM label on equipment is important. Token Ring is relatively expensive for the performance offered and, until recently, very proprietary to IBM. Token Ring provides IBM's solution for the larger connectivity picture as well, when PC LANs must be connected to IBM mini- and mainframe computers. New high speed token ring NICs offer 16-megabyte per second (Mbps) performance.

TRANSMISSION METHODS

Essentially, two methods used today transmit information along a network: the *token passing* method and the *collision avoidance/collision detection* method.

The *token passing* method uses an electronic token that is passed from one NIC to another in sequence. Think of it as a microphone being passed around in a group where a person may speak only when in possession of the microphone. Thus, in a token ring network, a network packet may be transmitted only when the NIC has possession of the token. The token passing system has proven to be a very efficient method of ensuring maximum performance and balancing the load in a network. Both ARCnet and IBM's Token Ring use this method.

NOTE: The words "token ring" can refer to three different things: 1) token ring can describe the method of transmitting packets of data; 2) it can refer to the IBM Token Ring NIC and other adapters that adhere to the IEEE 802.5 standard; and 3) it can refer to the actual Token Ring network operating system manufactured by IBM which runs with Token Ring NICs.

In a collision avoidance/collision detection system, each card transmits a packet whenever it wants. This system relies on a statistical assumption that under low or normal loads, relatively few collisions will occur. The second part of the scheme has the ability to recognize a collision when it occurs. When two cards transmit at the same time so that two data packets are passing through the network cable at the same time, a collision occurs. Neither the packet or corrupted packets are received. At these times, the system recognizes the collision and re-transmits the packets. As network loads get heavier and heavier, more collisions occur and more re-transmits are required. Of course, overall LAN performance goes down. **Ethernet** is the principal example of this type of system. The correct name for a collision avoidance/collision detection system is actually a *Carrier Sense Multiple Access/Collision Detection* system, which has the popular acronym CSMA/CD.

NETWORK OPERATING SYSTEMS

The heart of a network is the network operating system. Just as a personal computer won't function without an operating system, network hardware won't work without a *network operating system* (NOS). For the most popular type of personal computer used in business, the most commonly used operating system is MS/DOS — known as PC-DOS for real IBM PC users. For PC-based LANs, the most popular NOS is NetWare, manufactured by Novell, which has an estimated 65% market share.

Actually, you'll find a number of network operating systems available today in addition to NetWare. 3COM makes a NOS called **3Plus Open**, which is probably the second most popular system, with about a 10-15% market share. 3Plus Open runs under OS/2 and has been primarily designed to run with the 3COM's own Ethernet network cards. IBM also makes networking software to run with its Token Ring cards, with about a 10% market share.

The other major PC LAN NOS is **Vines**, manufactured by Banyan, which runs as a task under the Unix operating system. Vines has been a convenient way of implementing *Wide Area Networks* (WANs), which encompass more than what a locally cabled LAN can conveniently connect. Typically, a WAN connects LAN sights located throughout the country or even the world. Usually WANs require some type of dedicated leased telephone line or public data network, such as Tymnet or Telenet.

Both Banyan and 3COM formerly required proprietary server platforms and proprietary Ethernet NICs. With the pressure that Novell has been putting on the marketplace for cost effective, non-proprietary hardware-based networking, both Banyan and 3COM have opened up their systems in an effort to become more competitive.

Other network systems warrant mention because of their significance within narrow market niches. The first, **DECnet**, was designed by Digital Equipment Corp. (DEC) as an Ethernet-based network system for tying DEC minicomputers together and for allowing devices, such as terminal servers, to be handled over high speed Ethernet cabling. DEC recently released its DECnet Services for DOS (a.k.a. PCSA), which is an effort to allow DEC VAX minicomputers running the VAX/VMS operating system to provide file server functions for PCs on a LAN.

The **TOPS** network from Sun was one of the first to allow PCs and Apple Macintosh computers to share files on the same network. The PC implementation is a very simple rudimentary peer-to-peer networking scheme designed to provide low cost, low performance connectivity on PC LANs. Don't expect much more than file sharing from the PC version of TOPS because of its poor performance.

NET/OS, an interesting little network product, allows simple, low cost networking on a peer-to-peer basis. The interesting thing about NET/OS is that it can emulate some of the NetWare low-level network routines. For example, file locking schemes that work under Novell also work under NET/OS.

Finally, you'll find the third tier network systems such as **PC Office, ViaNet, Corvus Omninet,** and **10 Net.** These typically use proprietary NOS, which only work with the manufacturers' cards. There are also a host of so-called "slotless" LANS. *Slotless networks* do not require a NIC because they work over standard RS232 serial connections from the PCs' serial ports. While this provides extremely inexpensive "networking" it is also extremely slow.

NOVELL NETWARE

NetWare, a proprietary network operating system, was designed by Novell to run on PC-based network file servers. A number of things set Novell apart from the rest of the network operating system vendors.

First, Novell is committed to open architecture as it relates to hardware. Most early networks were designed to run the manufacturer's own NIC and NOS. While this was great for the manufacturer, it put customers at a significant disadvantage, because all hardware and software had to come from a single source. With Netware, virtually any NIC works. You can even mix hardware brands and topologies within a single network. You can use virtually any good 80286 and 80386 computer as a server and almost any PC as a workstation, even those that even remotely adhere to the IBM hardware standard. Even the DEC VAX (and soon most Unix machines) can work as file servers using NetWare for VMS or Portable NetWare.

Second, Novell has a commitment to performance. NetWare is renowned for its excellent performance. Using a whole suite of techniques—such as turbo FATs (indexed File Allocation Tables), elevator seeking, caching, and split reads (splitting read requests among two mirrored disks)—Novell has been able to significantly optimize network performance.

Third, Novell has a commitment to standards. The company has set its own standards by the sheer mass of the installed base of NetWare LANs. In addition, NetWare supports virtually all recognized NetWare standards. For example, NetWare has supported NETBIOS since the days when that was the only real PC LAN standard. Today, NetWare supports gateways to SNA, TCP/IP, the Macintosh file system, and a host of other standards. Soon, Novell will also support NFS.

NetWare comes in four major "flavors":

- **ELS (Entry Level System)** providing functionality for small networks

- **Advanced NetWare**, providing mainstream applications with high powered networking capability

- **SFT NetWare**, providing System Fault Tolerance

- **NetWare for VMS**, providing PC LAN services for the DEC VAX minicomputer running VAX/VMS

Novell's new products include *Portable NetWare*, which will run on Unix machines, and *NetWare 386*, the performance king of all NetWares.

Over time, as networking has matured, NetWare has garnered a larger and larger share of the networking marketplace. Surveys show NetWare with market shares of 55% to as high as 75% or more. Indications of the past and future direction of NetWare networking demonstrate that networks will increasingly become viable alternatives to mini- and even mainframe systems for many applications. The future of networking is bright.

HARDWARE BASICS

Three major hardware components make up a network system. The first is the NIC, which forms the interface between the workstation and the rest of the network. The *NIC* connects directly to a *network cable*, the second component of the network system, which is in turn attached to other workstations and a *file server*, the third component of the network system. The file server provides the management of shared network resources and maintains network hard disk drivers.

You'll find three major network systems in use today that use Novell's NetWare NOS—ARCnet, Ethernet, and Token Ring. You'll also find other proprietary network systems that can use the NetWare NOS, such as G-net from Gateway communications, Starlan from AT&T, Omninet from Corvus Systems, ProNet 10 from Proteon, and VLan from Networth. However, Ethernet, ARCnet, and Token Ring represent well in excess of 90% of the market for NetWare.

ETHERNET

Ethernet, clearly the worldwide standard for installed network nodes, has without a doubt more nodes installed worldwide than any other type of system. Ethernet is not only important for PC-based LANs, but also in the minicomputer and mainframe computer worlds. Ethernet is one of the major LANs used by the military. Ethernet provides the basis for DEC's DECnet LAN, the major interface used for TCP/IP LANs. In the world of the Unix operating system computer, virtually all networks are Ethernet based.

In the PC marketplace, you'll find Ethernet networks available from a wide variety of manufacturers, such as 3COM, Western Digital, Novell, Gateway, Tiara, Interlan, Ungermann Bass, and Excelan. You'll also find a flourishing Ethernet clone marketplace for PC NICs with some street prices close to the $100 level.

Ethernet, a linear bus network, has a standard defined by the Institute of Electrical and Electronics Engineers (IEEE) known as the 802.3 standard. (The IEEE is an international standards group which exists to formally define various standards. For example, the proposed twisted pair Ethernet standard has been designated 802.3 10 baseT; Token Ring has been defined as 802.5.)

You'll find three major hardware standards (actually two standards, with one emerging) for running Ethernet. The first uses thick Ethernet cable:

Thick Ethernet As its name implies, runs over a cable which is approximately one-half inch in diameter. Attachments made to the network bus cable use either *vampire taps*, a clamp-type device that punctures the cable and makes contact with the center core without requiring a splice, or an actual *physical* splice typically using N-type connectors. Each network bus cable attachment has a transceiver, which is in turn attached to a NIC. An Ethernet *transceiver* is a small device that provides the interface to the thick Ethernet cable. It connects to the NIC with a drop cable, also known as a *transceiver cable* or *AUI cable.*

Thin Net The second type of Ethernet also has the facetious name "cheapernet." Thin Net, actually *RG-58 coaxial cable*, is very much like television-style coaxial cable, but slightly smaller in diameter. Devices designed to work with Thin Net typically connect directly to the cable with a T connector and BNC fittings. *BNC connectors* are small bayonet-type connectors. In the PC world, virtually all thin net interface cards have an on-board transceiver to eliminate the need for the relatively expensive AUI cable and an external transceiver, because many external transceivers can cost as much as, or more than the Ethernet NIC itself.

Lattisnet The third semi-de facto standard for Ethernet provides a method that allows standard twisted pair telephone cable to handle the 10 megabyte-per-second (Mbps) Ethernet transmission rate standard. Lattisnet uses a device called a *concentrator* connected to each NIC, which makes Ethernet function like a traditional star-type network.

You'll also find other manufacturers, such as David Systems, that use a different approach to meeting Ethernet transmission requirements on twisted pair cabled Ethernet products. It is hoped that this whole situation, which allows incompatible Ethernet products, will change as soon as the IEEE 802.3 10base T standards gets defined. The 802.3 standard will define Ethernet specifications for 10 Mbps twisted pair wiring. To ensure fairness in the marketplace, none of the existing twisted pair schemes will be the standard. Reportedly, the new standard will be broad enough that most products can meet it and still be compatible with each other. When that happens, look for dramatic price reductions for twisted pair Ethernet products.

The basic parameters governing the design and implementation of Ethernet network systems follows:

Thick Ethernet

Segment length	1500 ft
Total cable length (including repeaters)	3000 ft
Maximum number of stations on a network	1024

Thin Ethernet

Segment length	600 ft
Total cable length	1800 ft
Maximum number of stations	100

ARCnet

ARCnet, undoubtedly the most significant network system without an IEEE standard, is a de facto network standard for many small, medium, and even large network systems. ARCnet, developed many years ago by Datapoint, quickly caught on with many manufacturers and network vendors. Standard Microsystems, one of the leading early ARCnet players, is still seen as one of the major ARCnet manufacturers. Like Ethernet, a myriad of manufacturers produce ARCnet NICs for PC-based networks. These include: Earth, Tiara, Network Innovations, Aquila, Compex, Thomas Conrad, ICE, Lantana, Novell, and others. Unlike Ethernet, ARCnet has only one standard. All NICs, with the exception of specialized server cards, use exactly the same protocols, shells, and software. Each ARCnet card is plug-compatible with any other ARCnet card.

ARCnet, which runs over standard RG-62 coaxial cable, uses hybrid topologies, as shown in Fig. 1-4. It uses token passing network protocols and bus topology. ARCnet can support fairly large networks. The maximum distance from any active device, NIC or active hub, to another is 2,000 ft. The maximum diameter of the network, the longest contiguous cable run, is 8000 ft (1 1/2 miles!). In fact, under NetWare, if you placed the server in the center of two ARCnet segments with an internal bridge, you could have an effective contiguous network 3 miles in diameter. Because ARCnet has a limit of 255 unique addresses, the largest contiguous ARCnet network can have 255 nodes.

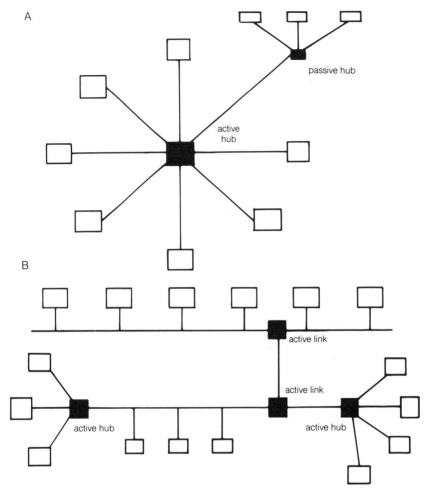

Fig. 1-4. Hybrid topologies. The file server can be located at any node.

Each active connection in an ARCnet network can be connected to a passive hub, which functions like a splitter in a cable TV installation. A *passive hub* has four ports, one in and three out. The published distance limit between passive hubs is 100 ft for each segment. Although in practice, distances of even less than 100 ft can often cause problems. We recommend that you limit the use of passive hubs as much as possible, because they greatly reduce network reliability.

Lately, ARCnet variations have emerged. The first, so-called *high impedance cards*, allow the network to be arranged in a segmented linear bus configuration with up to ten stations on each segment, which makes ARCnet look like Ethernet (from a cabling viewpoint). This variation has the advantage of minimizing the use of relatively expensive active ARCnet hubs.

The other ARCnet variant is a specialized Standard Microsystems card for use in ARCnet network file servers. The card, known as a *nodal priority card*, allows the file server to have access to multiple tokens during each trip along the network bus. Because the file server is the most active node on any network, it makes good sense to allow it more access to the token. Advertised performance increases approach 25% for this card.

ARCnet has proven an ideal NIC for small business networks with low to medium network loads. A disadvantage of this type of network, is that ARCnet interfaces are not widely available for mini-and mainframe computers. However, by using the NetWare NOS, you minimize this disadvantage, because Novell servers can bridge to other network topologies.

TOKEN RING

IBM is betting its connectivity future on the success of its Token Ring LAN. Token Ring LANs form a true ring topology that uses a token passing protocol for passing packets along the network. IBM's Token Ring LAN has a rated speed of 4 Mbps. Because it uses a token passing protocol, you would expect to see an effective bandwidth of 4 Mbps actually achieved. The IEEE 802.5 standard defines Token Ring as an international standard.

With interface cards currently available from NCR, Racore, Western Digital, and Proteon, as well as IBM, Token Ring is becoming a more readily available network interface. As more and more connectivity solutions depend on Token Ring as the interface of choice, expect to see more and more installations rely on Token Ring networks. Also, IBM has announced the availability of a 16 Mbps Token Ring card.

The hub of a Token Ring network, the *Multi-Station Access Unit* (MAU), has a number of connection points (usually 8) where cables to network stations are connected. Token Ring runs on a variety of cables. The standard cable is IBM Type 2, although Type 1, Type 3, and Type 6 can also be used. The general parameters for a Token Ring LAN are:

- A total length of 1200 ft.for the main ring.

- A maximum lobe length (distance from a MAU to a node) of 330 ft.

Repeaters can extend the lobe and ring distances. The actual distance parameters vary depending on the type of cable used.

SUMMARY

You'll find a wide variety of network hardware choices available today. The actual hardware that is best for a particular installation can vary widely, based on the specific factors and issues involved for that installation. At the risk of oversimplification, here are some broad generalizations that might help you in the selection of a LAN to fit your needs:

- ARCnet makes an excellent choice for small, self-contained networks, where low cost and high reliability are required.

- Ethernet works best for installations where multiple dissimiliar platforms, such as those that have the DEC VAX, Unix hosts, etc., or where there's already an existing Ethernet backbone.

- Because Ethernet provides greater transmission speeds than ARCnet, high performance installations will probably perform better with Ethernet.

- Token Ring is an excellent choice for "IBM shops," where IBM is firmly entrenched and direct connectivity to other IBM products, such as minicomputers and mainframes, is required.

- Because Novell supports multiple cards in a server, feel free to mix and match in complex environments.

2

NetWare Installation
Default Configuration

YOU'LL find installing Novell NetWare one of the more critical and time consuming tasks in implementing a network system. The exact installation process varies from system to system and from version to version, so you should refer to the specific documentation that comes with your version of NetWare to determine the exact way to handle each step. Every version of NetWare has an "Installation" manual that describes in great detail virtually every possible configuration and option.

This chapter covers installation basics by presenting a default installation process from start to finish. Subsequent chapters explore the custom installation process where you have the maximum amount of control over non-standard configurations for drivers, cards, printers, and other network resources.

Every NetWare installation, whether simple or customized, requires the following:

- Format and configure the physical hard disk drive (COMPSURF)

- Define the system configuration and install the hardware

- Link the operating system and utilities (NETGEN)

- Link the workstation shells (SHGEN)

- Install the network operating system and support files on the file server

GETTING READY

Before beginning the actual software installation, be sure to make working copies of each of the NetWare distribution disks. Effective with version 2.12, Novell no longer copy-protects distribution disks. Prior to that, the disk GENDATA had copy protection. Store the original disks in a safe place and always work with copies.

HINT: You'll find that the DOS utility DISKCOPY provides the best resource for copying distribution disks because it copies the disk label along with any subdirectory names. The disk label must to be on the disk. This is how the NETGEN process knows that the correct disk is in the drive when it needs it.

RUNNING THE INSTALLATION UTILITIES

Novell provides three methods for running their installation utilities: 1) you can run them directly from the floppy disks; 2) from a hard disk drive; or 3) if you're making multiple server installations or upgrades, you can run them from an existing file server.

In most cases, you'll find it best to use a hard disk drive to generate your operating system, shells, and utilities, because it saves considerable time and effort. If you elect to use the floppy disk method, you'll probably wear out your arm and the disk drive door, swapping floppy disks in and out.

In any case, start the network installation with the NETGEN floppy disk in Drive A:. Execute the program NETGEN. The opening screen on NETGEN asks whether you want to use the default configuration or a custom configuration (see Fig. 2-1). Usually, you can use the default configuration. Use the custom configuration if: 1) you want to use Resource Sets to ensure no conflict between server resources and network cards, 2) you want to use non-default configurations for your network cards, or 3) you want to use custom disk drivers (Value Added Disk Drivers (VADDs)).

Next, NetWare gives you the option of using floppy drives, a hard drive, or a network drive. If you select a hard drive or network drive, NETGEN looks for the presence of the installation files on the indicated disk. If not found, NETGEN prompts you through copying all of the floppy disks to the requested drive.

NETGEN automatically creates a directory structure made up of a subdirectory for each floppy disk's name. For example, the contents of

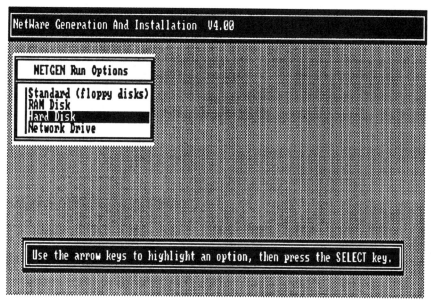

Fig. 2-1. The Opening screen of NETGEN.

the floppy disk named UTILEXE-1 gets copied to subdirectory UTI-LEXE-1. Most important, when you finish generating a LAN operating system, check that the files NetWare created during the installation process are copied to floppy disks for backup and safekeeping.

RUNNING NETGEN

At this point, if you have just completed uploading files to a hard disk, NETGEN loads the information from the GENDATA disk and brings up the configuration screen. If you are re-starting the installation process, you have to place the GENDATA disk in Drive A:.

NetWare stores your LAN's configuration information on the GENDATA disk. You have to use this disk whenever you modify your NetWare installation. Familiarize yourself with the current installation process shown in your NetWare Installation Manual. Because Novell upgrades their software on a regular basis, some specifics discussed here may no longer apply or may be implemented differently.

SELECTING NETWORK CONFIGURATION

The default NetWare installation has five items on the Select Network Configuration screen (see Fig. 2-2). The "Set Operation System Options" allows you to choose from available NetWare options, such as

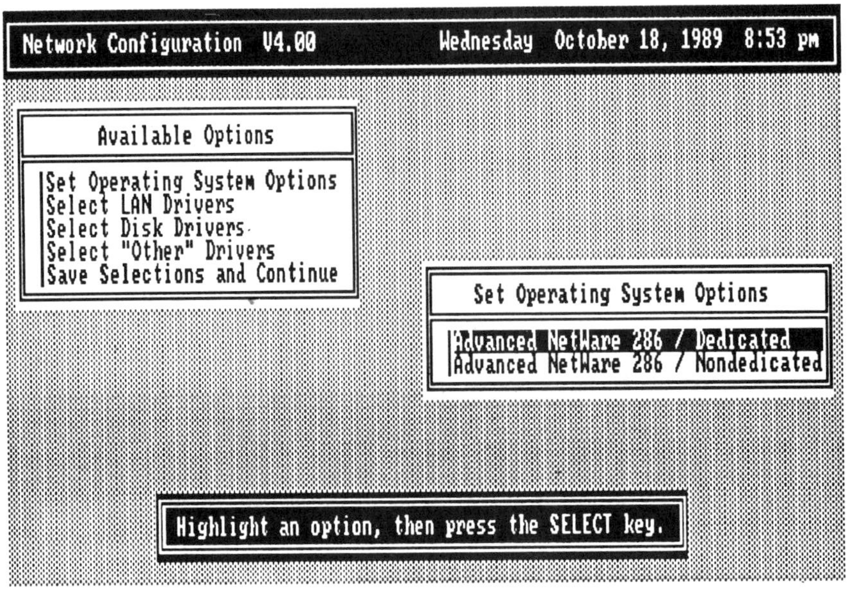

```
┌─────────────────────────────────────────────────────────────────┐
│ Network Configuration  V4.00        Wednesday  October 18, 1989  8:53 pm │
├─────────────────────────────────────────────────────────────────┤
│  ┌──────────────────────────────┐                                │
│  │       Available Options      │                                │
│  ├──────────────────────────────┤                                │
│  │ Set Operating System Options │                                │
│  │ Select LAN Drivers           │                                │
│  │ Select Disk Drivers          │                                │
│  │ Select "Other" Drivers       │                                │
│  │ Save Selections and Continue │                                │
│  └──────────────────────────────┘   ┌──────────────────────────┐ │
│                                      │ Set Operating System Options │
│                                      ├──────────────────────────┤ │
│                                      │ Advanced NetWare 286 / Dedicated │
│                                      │ Advanced NetWare 286 / Nondedicated │
│                                      └──────────────────────────┘ │
│                                                                   │
│           ┌─────────────────────────────────────────┐            │
│           │ Highlight an option, then press the SELECT key. │     │
│           └─────────────────────────────────────────┘            │
└─────────────────────────────────────────────────────────────────┘
```

Fig. 2-2. The Select Network Configuration screen.

TTS, Dedicated, or Non-Dedicated operation. The "Select LAN Driver" option allows you to tell NetWare which Network Interface Cards (NICs) your network uses. The "Select Disk Drivers" option choice allows you to specify the hard disk drive type options, such as MFM, DCB, SCSI, ESDI, etc. The "Select Other Drivers" allows for the use of other system specific drivers. Let's look at each of these in turn.

SETTING OPERATING SYSTEM OPTIONS

The Network Operating System (NOS) options in NetWare 286 allow you to run your LAN with either a dedicated or non-dedicated file server. Most of the time, you'll find it best to use a dedicated server. You can use a file server as a workstation with Advanced NetWare, however, this practice limits the performance of both the workstation and server functions, as well as raising serious issues about reliability. If your software locks up (crashes) the workstation/server and you re-boot from habit, forgetting that there are other users attached to it , you will crash the whole LAN. Therefore, we recommend that you do not use a non-dedicated server, except maybe for the very smallest of networks using NetWare ELS I or II.

If you are installing SFT NetWare, your NOS options allow you to use the Transaction Tracking System (TTS). TTS users can "back out" of a transaction to a known starting point in the event of a disk crash, power failure, or some other system disaster. However, your application software must be written to take advantage of TTS. Therefore, unless you have custom software that was designed with TTS in mind, configure your SFT NetWare for a standard SFT operating system.

Select LAN Drivers

Because NetWare can support a myriad of network interfaces, the NOS must know which NIC (or NICs) are in the server. Select the menu option select LAN drivers, which brings up a window giving three choices, "Select Loaded Item," "Load and Select Item," and "Deselect an Item." Choose Select Loaded Item and NETGEN gives you a list all of the currently available LAN drivers (see Fig. 2-3). Simply move the bounce bar to your card and hit the Enter key. The result is imilar to Fig. 2-4. If your server will have multiple NICs, select any other NICs at this point. When finished, press the Esc key to move on to the next step.

HINT: Be careful when you use either the Esc key or the Enter key because Novell is not consistent about their use.

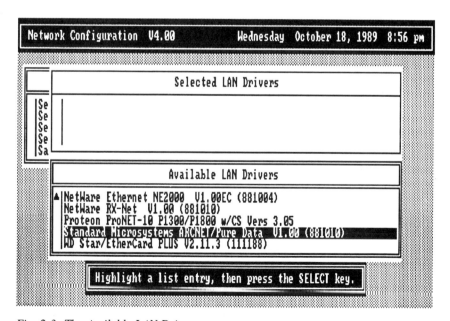

Fig. 2-3. The Available LAN Drivers screen.

Fig. 2-4. The Select LAN Drivers screen.

Select Disk Drivers

Again, Novell is an open-ended NOS that allows multiple hard drive sub-systems. You can use standard AT-type drives, PS/2 ESDI drives, SCSI drives, and drives attached to Novell Disk Co-Processor Boards (DCB). NetWare comes with a library of disk drivers. If you have a "non-standard" hard disk, the manufacturer should provide drivers for use with NetWare. The next chapter discusses loading these non-standard drivers.

At this point you will need to select the disk driver to be used from the standard list, shown in Fig. 2-5.

Select Other Drivers

Novell provides other drivers for use with NetWare. If you have systems in your server that require these drivers, load and configure them at this time. The manufacturer of these drivers will normally provide them with their products, along with specific instructions for their use.

Save Selections and Continue

When you are finished selecting your network interface card configurations and the drives to be used, you have to enter the file server information. Access the file server information screen by selecting the Save Selections and Continue option, as shown previously in Fig. 2-2.

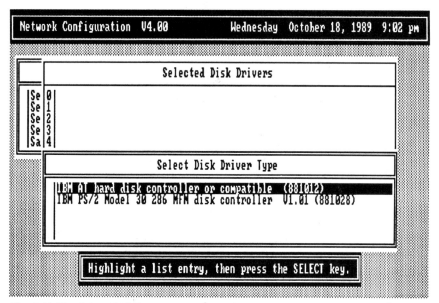

Fig. 2-5. The Select Disk Driver screen. The standard list of Driver types are included by Novell.

For each network card installed in the system, you have to assign a network address, which is simply a reference number to that file server. If there are multiple cards in a server, each card services a different network and must have a different address. Assign the same address to multiple servers servicing the same physical network.

Next you will get a screen that summarizes your selected configurations, as shown in Fig. 2-6. Review this screen closely to ensure that you have defined everything the way you desire. If the information is correct, press the Esc key and answer Yes to the question, "Continue with Network Generation using selected configurations."

NETGEN then links the operating system as you have specified. The linking process produces a file, NET$OS.EXE, that contains all of the selected parameters, along with disk and LAN drivers. As it generates your NOS, NETGEN also links and configures the NetWare utilities, such as COMPSURF, DISKED, VREPAIR and INSTOVL. This completes the generation of the NOS. The next step is to generate the LAN shells for workstations.

CREATING THE WORKSTATION SHELL (SHGEN)

LAN workstations use what is called a shell to communicate with servers. A *shell* is a small program that stays resident in workstation

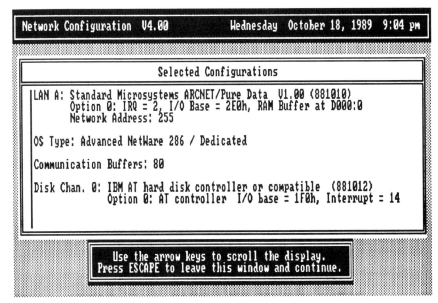

Fig. 2-6. The Selected Configurations screen. Be sure the definitions are correct before accepting them.

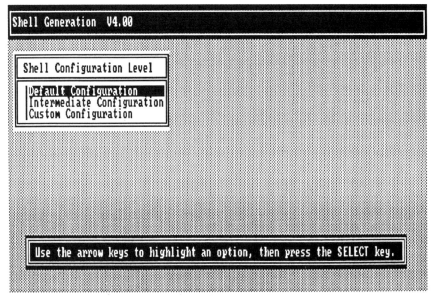

Fig. 2-7. The Opening menu for shell generation.

memory at all times, and provides the communication between the file server and the workstation.

You'll find the NetWare shell generation process fairly straightforward and, in fact, almost identical to the NOS NETGEN process just

described. Run SHGEN to bring up the opening menu for shell generation options (see Fig. 2-7). As with NETGEN, you have the option of
using a hard disk, floppy disk, or network server, and to use either the
default, intermediate, or custom configurations.

In all cases, the workstation shell must not conflict with any other
hardware in the machine. First, survey the resources present in the
machine or machines to be connected to the LAN. The manuals for each
I/O card, graphic card, hard disk controller card, etc. list the resources it
uses. If the Default option for the network card does not conflict with any
other resource, select the Default option. The "Default" option is discussed here and the "Intermediate" and "Custom" options in the next
chapter. Selecting Shell Configuration produces a bounce bar menu of
network interface cards that NetWare supports (see Fig. 2-8). Others are
also available, because drivers usually come with network cards. Place
the floppy disk shell containing the driver in a drive. SHGEN reads it and
automatically includes the driver on the list of available drivers.

Answer Yes to "Continue Shell Generation Using Selected Configuration?" (See Fig. 2-9). You will see the following messages on the

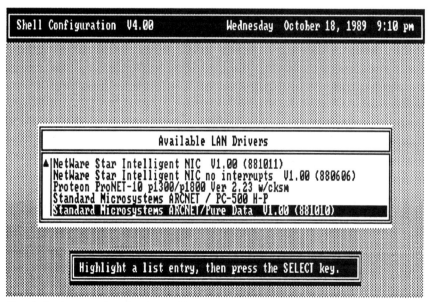

*Fig. 2-8. A menu of network interface cards is displayed when the Default option is
selected from the opening menu.*

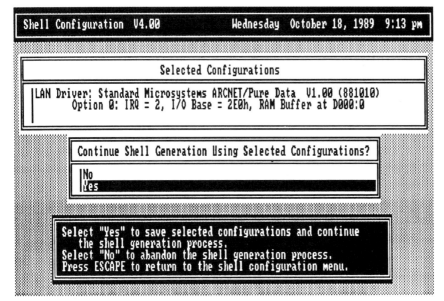

Fig. 2-9. The Selected Configurations screen.

screen as SHGEN finishes the process:

Novell Linker, Version 2.0
Linking SHGEN-2: IPX.COM.

Configuring SHGEN-2:IPX

The NetWare shell has two parts. The first, **IPX.COM**, contains the specific configuration for the network card. SHGEN links the configuration for each card used. The second part, **NET3.COM**, provides the communications link between MS/PC-DOS version 3.x and the IPX NOS communications driver. NetWare requires both parts so the shell can communicate with the server. Novell also provides NET2 and NET4 programs for those using DOS version 2.x and version 4.x, respectively.

This completes the necessary configuration and linking process. You are now ready to set up your file server and load the NOS.

LOADING THE NOS ON FILE SERVER

The final step in the installation of NetWare is actually loading the operating system and its associated files. With all of your network cards installed, your hard disk compsurfed, and your list of server resources created, boot your intended file server with DOS and run NETGEN.

NOTE: You might have purchased a disk that is already comp-surfed. In that case, you will not need to run the compsurf pro-gram. Do not worry if you haven't completed this step yet, NETGEN will check for you and take you to that subroutine as part of the installation process.

Notice that NETGEN keeps track of what you've already done. If you have completed all of the other steps, the bounce bar menu goes directly to the last item, NetWare Installation (see Fig. 2-10). If you have run the prior NETGEN options on a hard disk drive or another network drive, you will have already been prompted to save the files to a floppy disk. Do it again! Always complete this step!

The NetWare installation option first checks the physical configura-tion of the system itself. The program looks at what drives exist in the system, so that it can configure them properly (see Fig. 2-11). If you have not already compsurfed the disk, NETGEN returns you to this point in the process. You must compsurf the disk before you can install NetWare (see Fig. 2-12).

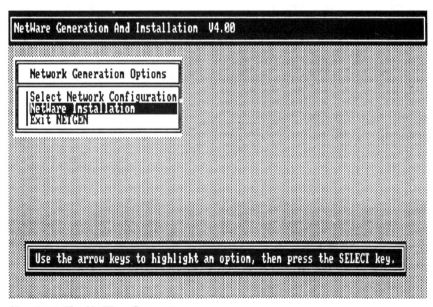

Fig. 2-10. The NetWare Generation menu.

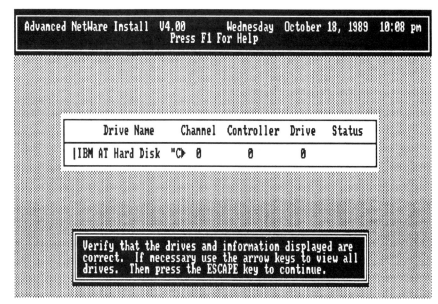

Fig. 2-11. Verifying the physical configuration.

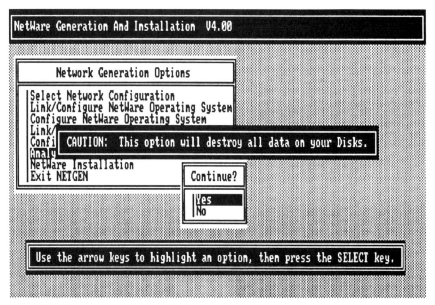

Fig. 2-12. The warning displayed when your disk has not been COMPSURFed.

COMPSURFING THE DISK

Compsurf is the Novell specific program that performs the low level format on the disk; places the Novell partition on the disk; and conducts an exhaustive surface and drive diagnostic process. As a general rule you should allow an entire night for the compsurf process to run when you select the recommended defaults.

You may elect to do an abbreviated test if you are pressed for time. This is not recommended. However, with the availability of the Novell HotFix capability, most latent disk defects will be caught and mapped out "on-the-fly."

FINISHING THE INSTALLATION

Under the default mode, NETGEN selects all of the installation options for you. Simply select the Select Default Installation Options from the Installation Menu. The rest of the installation proceeds on "auto pilot." Just follow the instructions on the screen and feed the floppy disks as requested. You have to answer a few questions during the process, such as "What is the file server name?" and "Which printers are used as network printers?" When asked if you want to install the NetWare files on the file server, answer Yes.

At this point, exit NETGEN. Re-boot the server and you should get a sign onscreen similar to the following:

```
Novell Netware        File Server Cold Boot Loader
(C) Copyright 1984,1987 Novell, Inc.  All Rights Reserved

Mounting Volume SYS
Initializing LAN A

Novell Advanced Netware 286 V.2.x   999999
All Rights Reserved

January 01, 1988
:
```

The colon (:) is the Novel Console Prompt. To familiarize yourself with the Novell Console Grid, type the command monitor. If your file server fails to boot, you may need to boot from a floppy disk. To do this, boot to DOS, then put the OSEXE-1 disk in A: and type NET$OS. It will load the contents of the first disk and then prompt you to put in the OSEXE-2 disk.

NOTE: If you are running off of a Novell DCB you will have to boot the file server using the floppy disk method.

3

NetWare Installation
Custom Configuration

CONSIDER the default installation procedures described in the last chapter as the shortest distance from the NetWare box to an operational server. This chapter explores the wide range of additional NetWare features and capabilities available by taking the custom installation route.

When you select Custom Installation from the NETGEN opening menu, you will notice a long menu. Because you are no longer just dealing with default configurations, there must be a flexible path to accomplish the steps in the network generation and installation process. A screen shot of the available options is shown in Fig. 3-1. This can be considered an outline of the steps that need to be accomplished and the order in which they should be done. So let's start at the top and select the Select Network Configuration option.

When you select this option from the NETGEN menu, the first thing that you notice is another long menu of options (see Fig. 3-2)—longer than in the default method. The NETGEN menu includes additional menu choices:

- Select Resource Sets

- Configure Drivers/Resources

- Edit

- Resource List

- Edit Resource Sets

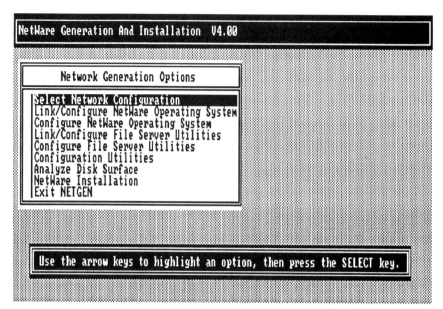

Fig. 3-1. Menu of Network Generation options available for Custom Installation.

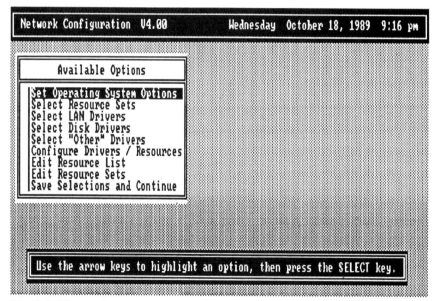

Fig. 3-2. The Available Options menu.

This menu allows you to define resources to ensure that conflicts do not occur between existing file server resources, such as ports and interface cards, and the LAN drivers — which is an important aspect of using the custom approach.

Using Resources and Resource Sets

Resources and Resource Sets merely provide a convenient way to track computer resources used versus those available. For example, a PC has a limited amount of interrupts and two devices cannot normally use the same interrupt—a computer resource. For example, if a serial port uses Interrupt 3, then neither the LAN driver nor a Disk Driver can use the same interrupt. If you select a resource set that already uses Interrupt 3, when the available LAN driver or disk driver configurations are presented, those that use Interrupt 3 will not show.

In pre-NetWare 2.1 days, LAN managers had to do all of the calculations manually to determine appropriate network settings—settings that would not conflict with other resources. They often found it difficult to know every occupied resource and other conflicts, especially in complex systems.

NetWare now comes with a fairly comprehensive set of pre-installed Resources and Resource Sets. The Novell software gives you a very straightforward method for adding your own resources to the list. *Resource Sets*, as you might guess, are merely collections of resources. Thus, you might define a Resource Set for a "Standard File Server" to consist of an AT-type machine with a standard MFM drive, LPT1, LPT2, COM1, and a Hercules graphics card. Then, when you select the Standard File Server Resource Set, it automatically uses those resources making up that set. Figure 3-3 shows a typical resource listing.

You can easily make a standard resource set. Then, if you get a new file server with a different configuration, all you need to do is manually change the individual resources that don't fit the standard set. Figure 3-4 shows the standard resource set for a Novell 386 file server.

To add a Resource simply hit the Ins key and follow the screen prompts (see Fig. 3-5). For I/O address ranges, simply enter the number of I/O address ranges, the starting address, and the range for each. For interrupt lines, enter the number of lines taken and the interrupt line number. Do the same for the DMA channel and memory segment address, which completes the Resource Set.

In actual practice, you identify the Resource Set (or all of the individual resources) first, then proceed to the selection of your LAN card configuration and disk drive configuration.

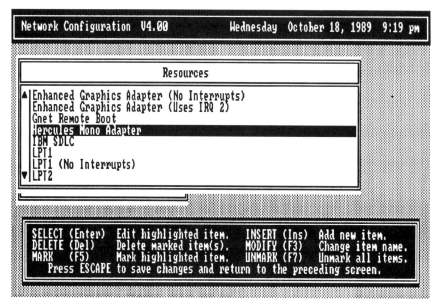

Fig. 3-3. A typical listing of Resources.

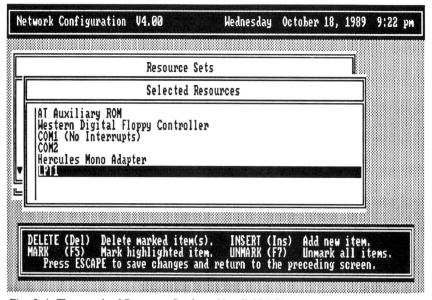

Fig. 3-4. The standard Resource Set for a Novell 386 file server.

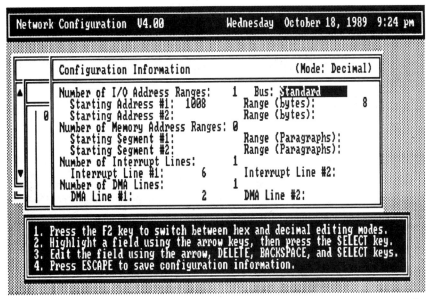

Fig. 3-5. Prompts listed at the bottom of the screen instruct the user in inserting the necessary configuration information.

Select LAN Drivers and Disk Drivers

The selection of a custom LAN driver and a disk driver works exactly the same as in the default method. The difference is that now you must configure the drivers. After you have selected all of your network cards and disk drivers, you must select the configuration that is to be used with the card. Unconfigured drivers are listed for you (see Fig. 3-6). Simply select each driver in turn, and choose the appropriate driver configuration.

The configuration screen for the LAN drivers is shown in Fig. 3-7. Notice that not all of the available options show up. This is because other server resources have already been selected which use those resources.

NOTE: Be sure to note the configuration you have chosen and set the switches and jumpers according to the manufacturer's specifications.

You may choose up to four LAN drivers for your server. After selecting the first LAN driver, simply hit the Ins key to bring up the list again and select an additional driver. Continue until you have selected all of the cards for your server.

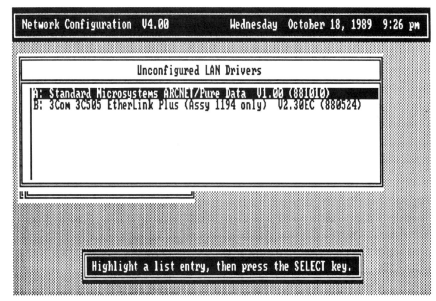

Fig. 3-6. Unconfigured LAN Drivers menu.

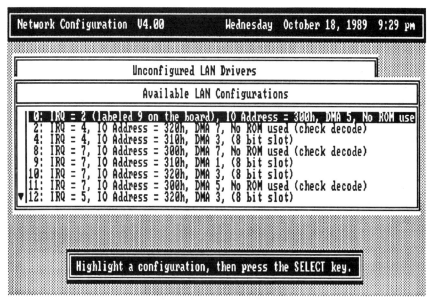

Fig. 3-7. The menu display for Available LAN Configurations.

The Selected Configurations screen, showing the use of Resource Sets is shown in Fig. 3-8. This screen gives a complete summary of the system. You should print or write its information on paper for future reference.

One final thing that you must do before proceeding to the linking phase of the NETGEN process: enter the file server information (see Fig. 3-9). For each network card in the server you will need to assign a network number. This is simply a reference number.

NOTE: If you are adding a second server to a physical network, the number must match the existing network. Otherwise, the number must be unique.

You will also be prompted for a number of communications buffers. Normally, you accept the defaults. If your installation is unique, you might want to adjust this number up or down based on the characteristics of your network. See the Novell manual for a detailed discussion on this parameter.

Under the Custom Method you must also tell the NETGEN program to link and configure the network operating system (NOS) and the File Server Utilities (see Fig. 3-10). When you are done, NETGEN will prompt you to download the files to a floppy. Be sure to do this step.

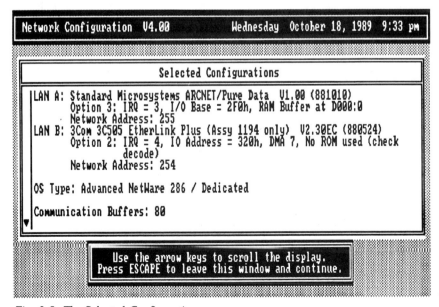

Fig. 3-8. The Selected Configurations screen.

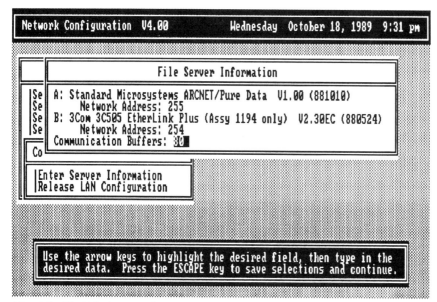

Fig. 3-9. The File Server Information screen.

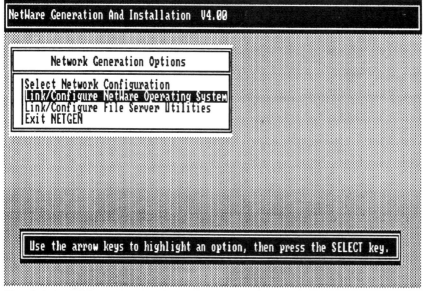

Fig. 3-10. Selecting the Link/Configure NetWare Operating System option from the Network Generation Options menu.

INSTALLING FILE SERVER HARDWARE

At this point, you must completely configure your file server. For each item write on paper the appropriate card and its installed configuration. Double check to ensure that the cards match the configuration you selected for your generation of the Operating System.

Disk Drives You may use a standard AT-type hard disk drives with a Western Digital controller or equivalent, the default configuration for AT and AT-compatible systems. You may also use standard ESDI drives, as used in the PS/2 series of computers. Novell provides support for SCSI drives using its Disk Co-Processor Board (DCB).

You may use specialty disk systems. For example, you might connect a DCB to an Adaptec 4070 disk controller, which is in turn connected to an RLL compatible drive, such as a Maxtor 1240.

Finally, you may also use third party disk systems using Value Added Drivers (VADs). For example, consider the use of a VAD for a Future Domain or Adaptec SCSI host adapter that is attached to a CDC Wren V drive. In releases prior to NetWare 2.1x, Novell did not allow third parties to independently develop disk systems and drivers. Consequently, available disk systems were limited and Novell controlled. Today, that situation is vastly better, because you can find VADs for the complete line of Novell products, except NetWare ELS I.

Network Interface Cards (NICs) Install all network interface cards at this point.

I/O Ports Install your serial ports (COM:) and parallel ports (LPT:) next. Each server may support up to two serial and three parallel ports. Be sure to write on paper the configuration you intend to use for the serial ports—baud rate, data and stop bits, parity, etc.

Graphics Cards Install your graphics card. We recommend a standard IBM monochrome or Hercules-compatible graphics card with a monochrome monitor for the server. Because you usually use the server for file services only, not as a workstation, don't tie up money for an expensive graphics system in the server.

Key Cards and UPS Monitoring Cards Earlier versions of Net Ware used a key card to protect from unauthorized copying and installation. Novell eliminated the need for this card with version 2.12 of

NetWare. Many key cards had on-board UPS Monitoring circuitry. A UPS is an *Uninterruptible Power Supply* or a battery backup device designed to provide emergency power to a file server in the event of a blackout or brownout. If you use UPS monitoring in your system, you might want to continue to use the key card, even though this is no longer necessary for proper operation.

Any Other Specialty Cards   Now, install any other specialty cards in your server. These cards may be, interfaces to tape drives or removable media.

CONTINUING WITH NETWORK INSTALLATION

The final step in NetWare installation is actually loading the network operating system (NOS) and its associated files. Run NETGEN again, this time from floppy disks on your intended file server. Notice that NETGEN tracks what you've already done. Therefore, you can do the configuration/installation process in several stages if you wish. If you have completed all of the other steps, the bounce bar menu goes directly to the last item, NetWare Installation.

NOTE: If you have been running the configuration/installation on your intended file server as a workstation attached to another file server, you may continue running it directly from this point.

The installation option first checks the physical configuration of the system itself. The program looks to see what drives exist in the system so it can configure them properly. You will be asked to verify the drive configuration, as shown in Fig. 3-11. If they have not been compsurfed, NETGEN will require that you do that here.

The actual installation procedure takes two steps. The first involves defining what you want to have done in the installation process. When each step is completed, the software sets a flag. The Custom Installation screen is shown in Fig. 3-12.

MISCELLANEOUS MAINTENANCE

The first menu item on the Miscellaneous Maintenance menu shown in Fig. 3-13, is "Load Operating System." This option allows you to set a flag to load the operating system. Note that nothing happens at this stage other than the setting of the flag. If you make a mistake at this point, you

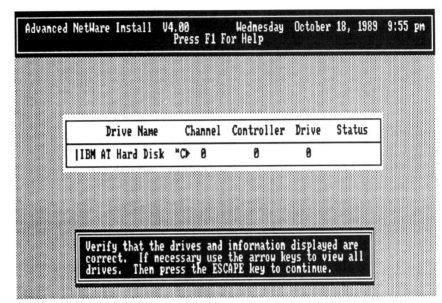

Fig. 3-11. The screen displayed for verification of the drives' configuration.

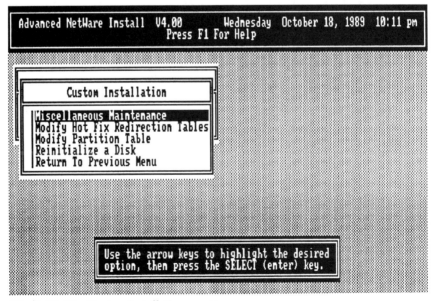

Fig. 3-12. The Custom Installation screen.

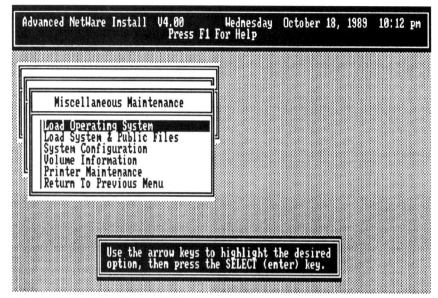

Fig. 3-13. The Miscellaneous Maintenance menu.

can back out. If the operating system has not already been loaded, set the flag here. The same holds true for "Load System" and "Public Files." If this is a first time installation or a NetWare upgrade, load these files. If you merely want to load a new operating system or change network card configurations, this procedure merely wastes time.

The "System Configuration" option on the Miscellaneous Maintenance menu lets you examine and change the system configuration. Likewise, the "Volume Information" option defines or changes the information about NetWare volumes present on the server. You can change the volume name, define the number of directory entries, and indicate whether to cache the directory, as shown in Fig. 3-14.

"Printer Maintenance," a very important part of the installation process, lets you define the network printers. In the case of parallel printers, you must choose whether to include it as a network printer. In the case of serial printers, you have to define the baud rate, parity, stop bits, and whether to use X-On/X-Off protocol.

Modify HotFix Redirection Table

This menu choice from the Custom Installation menu (refer back to Fig. 3-12) gives information about NetWare's HotFix feature. HotFix is Novell's basic level of fault tolerance which was available only in the SFT level of the software, but is now available in all versions of NetWare. As

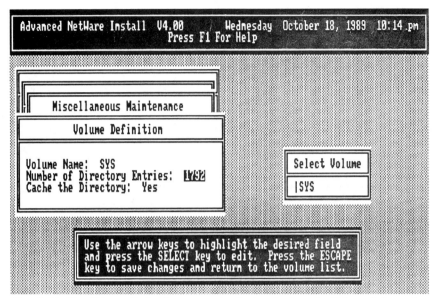

Fig. 3-14. The Volumn Definition screen is displayed when the Volume Information option is pressed from the Miscellaneous Maintenance Screen (Fig. 3-13).

its name implies, *HotFix* allows "fixing" minor disk errors as they occur, "on-the-fly." Whenever a disk is written to, HotFix re-reads the sectors and compares them to the memory image. If there is a fault, the area is locked and the HotFix Redirection area is used to hold the redirected write.

This menu choice not only shows a listing of the drives, their channel numbers, controller numbers, and drive numbers, but it also displays the logical and physical drive sizes and whether the disk is currently "Hot-Fixed" (see Fig. 3-15). Normally, the default HotFix area takes up 2% of the disk drive, a suitable size for the redirection area.

Modify Partition Table

The "Modify Partition Table" option, gives you the opportunity to control the partition sizes of your hard disk drives, which is important for large drives. For example, if you use a drive with a formatted capacity of 320 megabytes, you have several options when setting up the drive. The configuration you choose greatly depends on the anticipated-use profile of the system. You could use partitions of 250 MB and 70 MB, for example. Because NetWare has a 255 MB volume size limitation, you must split the drive into at least two partitions. Other options to consider might be two 160 MB partitions, or three 100 MB partitions and one 20 MB partition. This menu choice offers you the control to customize the hard drive partitions to suit your LAN's needs.

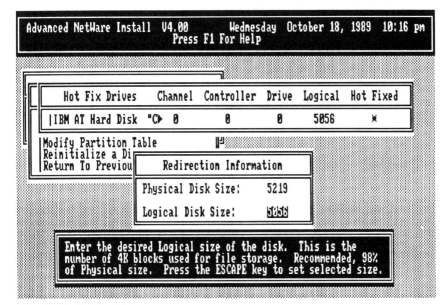

Fig. 3-15. HotFix drives screen.

INSTALLING THE SOFTWARE

At this point, you should have completed entering all the system parameters and set the appropriate flags for the actual installation. You can still back out at this stage. However, if you are ready to go on, answer Yes to the NETGEN inquiry about installing software and completing installation options on the server. Once you have selected all of the installation options, NETGEN will complete the process "hands-off," with the exception of hitting the Return key a couple of times when asked.

SHGEN

The NetWare shell generation process is fairly straightforward and executes the program SHGEN, which brings up the opening menu of shell generation options. Like NETGEN, you'll find options for generating hard disk, floppy disk, or network configurations, and for using Default, Intermediate, or Custom configurations. The Default was discussed in the last chapter, so let's look at the differences in the "Intermediate" and "Custom" options.

In all cases, the network shell must not conflict with any other hardware in the machine. First, do a survey of the resources present in the machine or machines to be connected to the LAN. The manuals for each

I/O card, graphic card, controller card, etc. list the machine resources used.

Beginning with version 2.1x, NetWare uses configurable shells. Prior to that, only one option was available for shells, which meant that, if a conflict occurred, the other card, or cards, had to be changed. Unfortunately, you frequently didn't have the option and you had to change your hardware.

Intermediate Configuration Option

The "Intermediate" Option allows the configuration of the network shell. After selecting the LAN driver from the list of drivers, you can choose from among the available configurations for that particular card. You would want to use this option when you need to change the default configuration of a network card in the workstation in order to avoid a conflict, but you do not need the added burden of full blown Resource Sets.

Custom Configuration Option

The "Custom" Option allows you to use Resource Sets, just like the custom version of NETGEN. Use this option to assist in finding an available LAN Shell configuration in a heavily loaded workstation. Tracking all the resources in use can be difficult, particularly when your LAN uses exotic graphics cards, specialty communications cards, or other unusual cards.

Linking IPX

The final step of the shell generation process is to link the appropriate IPX LAN communications driver. The NetWare shell consists of two parts. The first, **IPX.COM**, contains the specific configuration of the network card, which gets linked for each card configuration used. The second part, **NET3.COM**, provides the communications link between PC/MS-DOS 3.x and the IPX driver. Because individual items can vary from operating system to operating system and from version to version, consult your manual for details.

After the installation process finishes, exit NETGEN, re-boot the server, and you should get a sign on screen similar to the following:

```
Novell SFT Netware     File Server Cold Boot Loader
(C) Copyright 1984,1987 Novell, Inc.  All Rights Reserved

Mounting Volume SYS
Mounting Volume VOL1
```

Initializing LAN A
Initializing LAN B

Novell Advanced Netware 286 V.2.11 999999
All Rights Reserved

January 01, 1988
:

SUMMARY

The "Custom Installation" option of NetWare is designed to provide the user with the most flexible method possible for configuring, installing and modifying the NetWare operating system. While seemingly complex and involved, the user interface of the two installation programs, NETGEN and SHGEN, provide a well structured, "point-and-shoot/fill-in-the-blank" method of getting your system up and running. Hopefully, these first two chapters have given you the procedural overview necessary to complete your own NetWare installation.

Disk Manager Novell

DISK Manager Novell, from Ontrack Computer Systems, is a software utility that you can use to install hard (fixed) disk drives on NetWare file servers without the use of Novell's COMPSURF program. The Ontrack software can provide extra benefits particularly when you use non-standard disk drives. *Non-standard drives* are those that do not exactly match the drive table that comes in a computer's ROM setup system. Also, Disk Manager Novell (DMN) can make the installation process go substantially faster than COMPSURF.

USING DISK MANAGER NOVELL

To set up any hard disk drive, you must initialize it with a low-level format, partition it, and then perform a high-level format on it. DMN provides a convenient, menu-driven process for all these steps. The program also provides an automated process for installing a disk drive. For most installations, this automated process will be the most appropriate and simplest way to go. The software's menu-driven approach provides the most control with its sequential handling of each step.

To proceed with the automated method, simply decide which of six available situations apply to your installation. The choices are: 1) one or two drive installations, 2) first or second drive installations, and 3) standard or non-standard installations.

For sake of illustration, let's assume a simple one drive installation, where the drive is the first one in the computer system and it is a standard drive. Simply type the command DMN SETUP04 to initiate the automated installation process. The SETUP options are explained in detail in the manual, and are beyond the scope of this book.

The automated process pauses periodically to prompt for information needed to complete the process. The major data DMN needs is the bad block information. Regardless of the method used, you will need to enter data from the hard disk's *bad block table*. Almost all drives larger than approximately 70 or 80 MB have a number of bad blocks, which is completely normal. *Bad blocks* are merely minor defects in the surface of the disk platters that prevent information from being reliably written to those areas. However, bad block data is so important that it is always affixed to the top of the drive at the factory in a "factory bad block table."

Your hard disk drive may also develop additional bad blocks, which can come from wear, rough handling, "head crashes" or other problems. Before you perform the hard disk initialization or low-level format, you must enter the data from the bad block table on the drive to ensure that these portions of the disk are never used. Additionally, your software should test the disk as the initialization is performed to map out any new bad blocks that are not on the factory bad block table. A bad block's location is defined by its head and cylinder numbers.

For many installations you'll find it desirable to manually install DMN. Let's look at a sample manual disk initialization using Disk Manager Novell in the manual mode. We assume a standard AT-type machine with a 72-megabyte hard disk drive that has 8 heads and 1024 cylinders.

First, install the disk drive in the machine following the manufacturer's instructions. Then, to tell the machine that the drive has been installed, you need to enter the drive's parameters with the SETUP routine. You'll find SETUP either contained within the machine's ROM and accessible when the PC is booted, or SETUP may come from a floppy disk. Either way, follow the computer manufacturer's instructions. Make sure that the drive's heads and cylinders, as installed in SETUP, match the actual number in the drive—in this case, 1024 by 8.

Re-boot the machine with DOS and run DMN. The Opening menu of Disk Manager Novell is shown in Fig. 4-1. Select the (I)nitialize option from the Main menu. The first step in initializing a drive, is to enter the bad block table. Select (D)efect list management and follow the instructions for entering each of the factory bad blocks.

Next select the (I)nitialize option, which gives you the option to initialize the entire disk, a track on the disk, or a single partition. Select (D)isk.

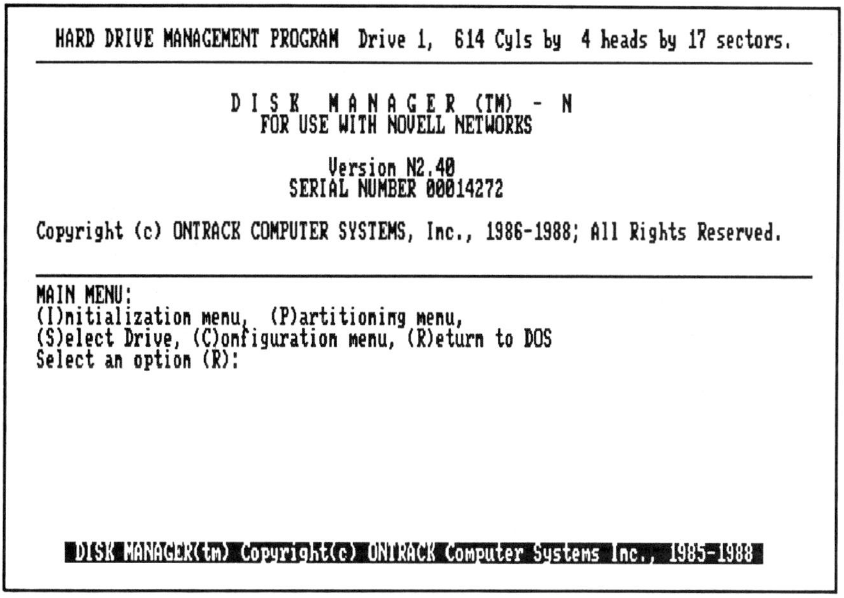

```
┌─────────────────────────────────────────────────────────────────┐
│                                                                   │
│    HARD DRIVE MANAGEMENT PROGRAM  Drive 1,  614 Cyls by  4 heads by 17 sectors. │
│                                                                   │
│              D I S K   M A N A G E R  (TM)  -  N                   │
│                    FOR USE WITH NOVELL NETWORKS                    │
│                                                                   │
│                         Version N2.40                             │
│                      SERIAL NUMBER 00014272                       │
│                                                                   │
│    Copyright (c) ONTRACK COMPUTER SYSTEMS, Inc., 1986-1988; All Rights Reserved. │
│                                                                   │
│  ───────────────────────────────────────────────────────────     │
│    MAIN MENU:                                                     │
│    (I)nitialization menu,  (P)artitioning menu,                   │
│    (S)elect Drive, (C)onfiguration menu, (R)eturn to DOS          │
│    Select an option (R):                                          │
│                                                                   │
│                                                                   │
│                                                                   │
│                                                                   │
│                                                                   │
│   ██DISK MANAGER(tm) Copyright(c) ONTRACK Computer Systems Inc., 1985-1988██ │
│                                                                   │
└─────────────────────────────────────────────────────────────────┘
```

Fig. 4-1. Main menu for Disk Manager Novell.

Next, DMN prompts you to enter the interleave value. The *interleave setting* allows you to optimize disk access speed. Many hard disks spin too fast for the controller to read to disk each sector in succession. If a disk does not have time to read a particular sector, the unit must wait for the disk platter to finish one complete revolution for the sector to come back around to be read.

The *interleave value* is simply the number of revolutions of the disk required to read an entire track. An interleave value of two means that every other sector is read as the disk spins, or two revolutions are needed to read an entire track. An interleave of three means one sector is read, followed by two that are skipped. An interleave of one, also called 1:1, provides the fastest data transfer rates, but only if the controller can handle the data fast enough for this setting. You'll find the disk performs better with a conservative interleave rather than one that forces the controller to do repeated re-reads because the interleave number is too low. The standard interleave value for a standard AT-type controller with a standard AT-type hard drive is three.

Disk Manager Novell warns you that all data will be completely destroyed by the initialization process. If this is not a new drive, ensure that all important data on the drive has been backed up and answer Y to continue with the low-level format process. DMN then initializes the disk and tests (verifies) its surface for defects. The verification process

searches for any unmarked bad blocks. DMN also has a (V)erify option
that allows you to re-run the verification process at any time the need
arises.

PARTITIONING THE DISK

In the next step, you must partition the disk. A hard disk drive can
have different types of partitions: PC/MS-DOS, Read/Write, Xenix,
NetWare, and others. As the name implies, a *partition* allows you to use
the disk for multiple processes or multiple operating systems. Select the
(P)artitioning menu option from the Main menu.

For this example, simply select the (N)ew partition table and then use
the default table to give a 72-megabyte NetWare partition using all the
cylinders on the disk. The partition process allows other options for
advanced disk setups, which include selecting a boot partition, deleting a
partition, defining the partition type, and defining starting and ending
cylinders.

After you partition the hard disk, you have to perform a high-level
format. Select the (P)reparation option from the DMN Main menu and
choose (S)can Network Partition from the sub-menu. As with the initialization process, scan destroys any data on the disk. You can run Scan multiple times and, time permitting, you should run it overnight on a new
system to ensure proper operation of the drive under the demanding conditions of a busy LAN.

The final step in getting a disk ready for LAN use, is to execute the
NetWare installation program. Be sure to skip the compsurf portion of the
process, because Disk Manager Novell totally replaces the COMPSURF
program.

ADVANCED FEATURES

If your LAN has a non-standard hard disk drive, you have to prepare
a special configuration file for DMN. Many configuration files are
already included on the DMN distribution disk, so this step may have
been done for you by Ontrack Systems. The configuration file is a one
line ASCII file containing the non-standard disk's parameters. The file for
a Maxtor 1140 drive might have this data:

    918, 15, 0, 65535, 11, 13, 12, 180, 40, 0, 17

The parameters are (in order): number of cylinders, number of heads,
reduced write current start, write precomp start cylinder, ECC correction

length, control byte, standard timeout value, format drive timeout value, check drive timeout value, landing zone cylinder, sectors per track. Most of these values do not apply to a standard AT-type machine, so this is an easier process than it might seem at first glance.

We have used Disk Manager Novell for a number of years to assist in the setup and configuration of LAN disk drives. With many non-standard and alternative drive types, such as ESDI and SCSI drives, you may find that Disk Manager Novell is the only way to prepare these drives for use with Novell networks.

DMN has also proven itself very useful for testing and verifying drives that have been in service for a while and that are showing signs of unreliable or questionable operation. Disk Manager Novell is very straightforward, very reliable, and about as easy to use as any disk setup program we've seen.

SUMMARY

Disk Manager Novell is an important disk utility that has proven itself to be of great value in the Novell environment. Although you will find COMPSURF entirely adequate for the vast majority of installations, you also will find that if you need the capability of DMN, you will not be able to get along without it.

PART II

Security and Accounting

5

NetWare Security

SECURITY can have several meanings, depending upon the individual. As applied to LANs, the word can mean data integrity through *hardware* fault tolerance, *operating system* fault tolerance or *application* fault tolerance. It can also have the traditional meaning restricting users from accessing data. *Fault Tolerance* is the ability to keep the system running even though a piece of the system has failed. NetWare lets you accomodate the operating system and hardware, and gives programmers the tools to incorporate fault tolerance into application programs. Many applications are written specifically for NetWare, (Da Vinci's eMAIL, for example) and actually use NetWare to control their security. This chapter discusses the hardware aspects of security. Then, it discusses how NetWare and you, as the LAN manager, can control your system.

HARDWARE SECURITY

NetWare allows different levels of fault tolerance, depending on the importance of your data. All versions of NetWare 2.1 include Redundant Directory Structures and Power Up Verification, Read After Write Verify, and HotFix. If the Read After Write Verify returns a bad sector, NetWare's HotFix marks that sector as faulty and writes the data to another part of the disk.

SFT (Software Fault Tolerant) NetWare also has advanced security features such as Disk Mirroring, Disk Duplexing, and Novell's Transaction Tracking System. *Disk Mirroring* maintains duplicate data on two identical disk drives. If one drive fails, the second drive continues running without any data loss or corruption.

Disk Duplexing takes disk mirroring one step further by allowing the presence of two disk controllers, one controlling each mirrored drive. With Disk Duplexing, if the failure is in the controller, the system continues operating without interruption.

Application software can also use Novell's Transaction Tracking System (TTS). Let's consider an accounting system transaction that makes several disk writes to update different database files. The accounting software updates the payables database, then the server crashes before the system can write to the general ledger database. The result, of course, is that you have a serious accounting problem. With TTS, if only part of a transaction completes before a "data accident," SFT NetWare backs out of the transaction when the system returns to operation, as if it had never been entered. You may have to reenter the data, but that's infinitely better than corrupted or bad data.

UPS SYSTEMS

Uninterruptable Power Supplies (UPS) are also part of fault tolerance. A UPS ensures that in case of a power fluctuation, or loss, that power is maintained to the server. If power is ever lost to the server you could risk losing data and possible damage to the system. Novell SFT NetWare supports the monitoring of UPS devices to signal the server if power has been interrupted. This is provided via their UPS monitoring board or a DCB located in the server with a cable running to the UPS. When power is disturbed, the UPS signals users on the network of the failure and alerts them to log out before power is completely lost.

Several companies make UPS devices compatible with Novell. Elgar was the first certified and probably the most innovative. They have produced value-added programs that run on the server and will talk interactively with the UPS. This allows the UPS to know when the server has shut down and to shut itself off through a process called *Invertor shutdown*. With this process the UPS does not completely drain its batteries when power is lost, which causes unneeded run down of the unit.

DATA SECURITY FOR USERS

The main focus of this chapter gives you enough information to intelligently give system access to those who need it, while keeping out unauthorized users. With all data located in a central place, you'll find it important to have a good grasp on this concept before your system has any data. First, let's look at the way NetWare handles security.

To begin, let's examine LAN security from a user's point of view. When a user logs a workstation onto the network, the machine loads the IPX and NETx shells to access the LAN. After these shells load, the user can change to the network drive, most commonly the F: drive, and execute the directory command. The user sees two executable program files, Slist and Login. The user can run these programs, but cannot delete them or write data to a network drive.

When the user runs the Login program, it asks for a login name and a password. Once both are entered, a NetWare user runs the System login script and the user's personal login script (if applicable). Login then exits the user to a menu system, if one has been installed, or to the DOS prompt.

Without any access rights, a user can only read data from the Public and Login directories. Even though a user hasn't been given rights to other directories, they can change to those directories. However, the user will only see an empty directory if they try to look for a file. At this point, the user best logout, because without access rights, a LAN is worthless.

We strongly believe every LAN must have security protection. Networks without security don't prompt for a password; all users have total access to the system, without inhibitions. If a hostile user logs on as a supervisor, think of the damage they could wreak. All data could be lost — or even worse, replaced with data that could damage more than just the LAN. To better understand NetWare security, let's take a brief look at how the software tracks users and their security.

THE BINDERY

NetWare maintains a database of all resources and users known to the LAN, called the *Bindery*. The Bindery contains detailed information about users, such as their password, accounting balance, groups belonged to, and access restrictions on the network. The Bindery also keeps information about other servers and applications that may use the bindery for access to the network services.

The Bindery treats each user as an object with an associated set of properties. For example, the Bindery may contain the object Supervisor, which may have the properties PASSWORD, SECURITY_EQUALS, GROUPS_I'M_IN and IDENTIFICATION. Each of these items may be an individual item or set of items.

ACCOUNT CHECKUPS

NetWare employs half-hour security checks. That is, every half-hour, the Novell software checks each workstation to ensure it has the proper server rights. If the account has expired, the accounting balance has run out, or the account has been disabled, NetWare asks the user to log out. The software informs the user that access has expired and they will be cleared from the network in five minutes. NetWare gives one more warning when one minute is left, before clearing the user from the network.

SETTING UP SECURITY

With that bit of background, let's look at how NetWare implements security. Log in to your system as supervisor. Type SYSCON, press the Enter key, and NetWare brings up the system configuration menu utility. This utility sets up and maintains "resource accounting" (more on that later); retrieves information about the file server; sets up users and groups; and sets up supervisor functions on the network. Select User Information to bring up the User Names currently defined on your system. For this example, create a new user. To create a new user, press the Ins key. SYSCON prompts you for a user name, which can be up to 47 characters long.

NOTE: The user name *may not* contain spaces, slashes, backslashes, colons, semicolons, commas, asterisks, question marks, or tildes.

After you define the user name, go to the User Information menu screen, which controls all the security and resource accounting information about this user (see Fig. 5-1). If resource accounting has been installed, the first item will be "Account Balance,"which is used in NetWare's accounting systems and is discussed in the next chapter. "Intruder Detection" also requires that accounting be installed, which is discussed, along with other items, next.

Account Restrictions

Under "Account Restrictions" is a list of various constraints you can place on users. You can set up defaults for these values from the supervisor menu in SYSCON. You set individual user's settings from that user's Account Restrictions menu. Figure 5-2 shows the Account Restrictions screen.

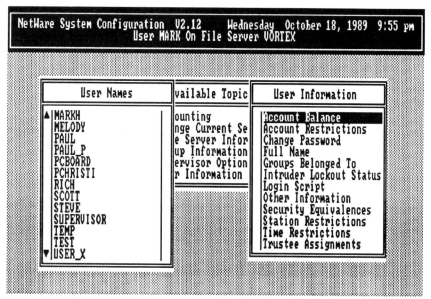

Fig. 5-1. The Use Information menu.

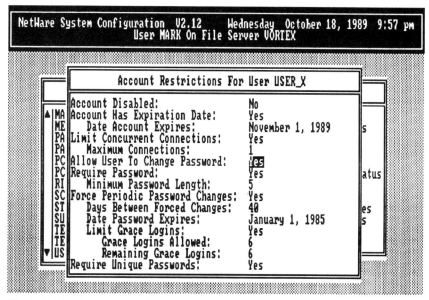

Fig. 5-2. The Account Restrictions screen.

Account Disabled   You can give a user no log in capability, yet maintain their account and properties on the server. As supervisor, you can set "Account Disabled" to yes, so the user is informed that the account has been disabled by the supervisor. Then, NetWare denies access to the user. If the user is logged onto the LAN at the time the account gets disabled, the user is informed of the supervisory action and logged out at the next half-hour security check.

Account Has Expiration Date   Occasionally, you might want to set up a temporary user, maybe for a visiting worker from another office or a temporary employee with a fixed employment period. If you specify an expiration date, the user cannot log in after that date. If a user tries to log in to an expired account, they find the account disabled.

Limit Concurrent Connections   NetWare allows a user to log in at the same time from as many workstations as they want. Sometimes, for security reasons, you might want to allow a user to log only from a single station at a time. You can set this between 1 and 100.

NOTE: If you use the standard NetWare shell, then Quarterdeck's DESQview, Microsoft's Windows, and Macintosh's Multifinder will each make only one connection for all sessions. The OS/2 Requestor and PCMos with the NetWare PCMos shell (and possibly some special releases of the DESQview and Windows) can make more than one connection per session.

Allow User to Change Password   If you have a public account where everyone knows the password, you might not want a user to be able to use such a password. If you set this option to no, only the supervisor can change the accounts password.

Require Password   When first installed, NetWare does not require a password for any user. When installed and running, we strongly recommend you change this option. You can set it for any length between 1 and 20 characters, which lets users input their own password when logging in for the first time. If you don't set this option, your LAN really has no security.

NetWare will default to a five-character password. Longer passwords are more secure, but are harder to remember, more likely to be mistyped, and take more time to enter. Shorter passwords are easier to guess and less secure.

Force Periodic Password Changes You'll find it a good security precaution to have users change their password at regular intervals. You can set this option to force such changes.

Days between Forced Changes. This uses days and defaults to 40. If this value is too short, it becomes a nuisance and users can forget their passwords. If this value is too long, it loses its security value.

Date Password Expires. Users are forced to change their password on this date, which is recalculated every time users change their password.

Limit Grace Logins. When users do not change their password within the specified period, you can allow a grace period for a specified number of logins before declining access. Users are advised that passwords have expired; they get prompted to change their password. If after the last grace login, passwords have not been changed, these delinquent users are locked out of the system. Their accounts are disabled after the last grace login. If grace logins are not limited, users are prompted to change their password every time they log in. But they are never denied access because a password has expired.

Require Unique Passwords NetWare can remember the last 8 passwords that a user has employed. If you choose to require unique passwords, a user cannot change to a password they have not used for the last 8 changes. If you choose not to require unique passwords, a user can use the same password over and over again, which lessens security.

Change Password

We recommend that you, as supervisor and LAN manager, assign each user a password when you create their account. Because passwords are irreversibly encrypted by NetWare, nobody can ferret out a user's password—even the supervisor. If a user forgets a password, you can only grant them access to the system again, by giving them a new password.

Full Name

Full name is a text field used for reporting purposes only. Some utilities let you print the full name field rather than the login name so you can be more descriptive on reports.

Groups Belonged To

Groups provide a way to organize your LAN into subsets, such as Accounting, Marketing, Administration, or other departments that might need access to specific directories and files as a work group. When you first set up groups, NetWare automatically makes all users part of the group "everyone." Each group can have its own security system. Users may belong to multiple groups. Groups are discussed in greater detail later in this chapter.

Intruder Lockout Status

If resource accounting is installed on the server, NetWare's Intruder Lockout function lets you detect and lockout an account after a determined number of incorrect login attempts. You can view the status of this account from this menu option. You can maintain the bad login try record for a designated amount of time, so when NetWare detects the intruder, their account can be locked for a specified period of time. This intruder detection is enabled using the supervisor menu in SYSCON.

Login Script

You'll find login scripts a good way to implement individual security environments. If you don't want users left at the DOS prompt so they can play with files, you can force them to use a menu system after executing the login script. Login script commands are covered later in this book.

Other Information

This option gives you general information about every user. It tells you the time each user last logged into the server and whether the user is a file server console operator. A *console operator* has privileges that normal users don't have—such as, to operate FCONSOLE and some of the other NetWare utilities. This option also shows the disk space currently in use. Even if you don't use resource accounting, you'll sometimes find this information useful. This option will also tell you the users bindery ID number, which is useful for determining users' mailbox directories in the SYS:MAIL directory.

Security Equivalences

NetWare may assign a user's security because of a group belonged to, or because of an association with another user. You might want to set up a word processing group with access to the WP directory. You may also want to give secretaries the same rights as the person they work for to allow both to work on the same documents. A user with the equivalence of another user has the same rights as the latter. More on this when groups are discussed.

You may also grant SUPERVISOR equivalence to a user who co-administers the system. The co-administrator has supervisor rights, and cannot use their own name to supervise the system.

Station Restrictions

You can assign a user Station Restrictions, so that a person can only log on to the server from their specified workstation. You'll find this useful for installations with diskless workstations, where you don't want users to log on to the server and download data to a floppy disk. This option also limits users accessing data from workstations located in isolated areas.

Time Restrictions

Along with Station Restrictions, you can place a time restriction on users so they don't try to break into data files after hours. Figure 5-3 shows the Time Restrictions screen.

Trustee Assignments

Trustee assignments or trustee rights represent the heart of NetWare security. NetWare uses these assignments to designate what access a user

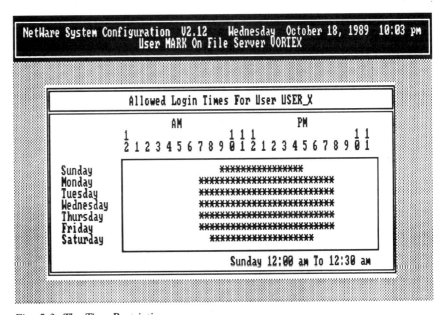

Fig. 5-3. The Time Restrictions screen.

has to files and directories. You set up user trustee assignments with SYS-
CON and individual directory rights with FILER. Trustee assignments
consist of:

- Read from files

- Write to files

- Open existing files

- Create new files

- Delete files

- Parental rights

- Search for files

- Modify file name/flags

Figure 5-4 shows an example of setting up these rights with SYSCON.
Most NetWare rights' names describe their functions adequately, but you
may find Parental and Search rights a bit difficult to grasp. *Parental rights*
give users the ability to create subdirectories, delete subdirectories, and
modify directory rights masks. *Search rights* allow users to see file names
in a directory. Without search rights, a user must enter the complete and
exact file name to access that file.

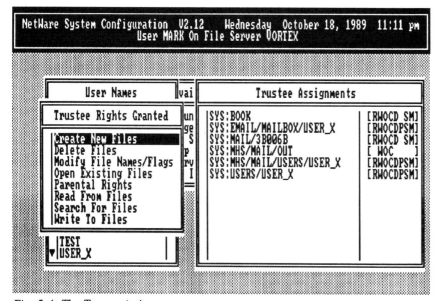

Fig. 5-4. The Trustee Assignments screen.

A user may have any combination of rights. NetWare provides its greatest security through special combinations of user rights. You'll find some combinations used very frequently with NetWare. The Novell program abbreviates rights by using their first letter and uses the figure [RWOCDPSM] to abbreviate security assignments. For example, [ROS] shows Read (R), Open (O) and Search (S), which is the public directory, the default. This combination gives a user access to look at, and search for all the file names, open the files for access and read from any file.

True NetWare security comes from combining these rights for various users as needed. For example, when you install an application on the LAN, you give users Read, Open and Search rights into the directory that contains the executable files. However, you may decide not to give them write, or deletion rights, in case they accidentally delete or overwrite a program file. You'll probably also want to give all users rights to their own personal subdirectory, for example, SYS:USERS \ JOHN.

NetWare uses a hierarchial security structure. Thus, a user's rights cascade down to the subdirectories below, which means a user with [ROS] rights in the SYS:PUBLIC directory also has [ROS] rights in the SYS:PUBLIC \ APPS directory. You can block this cascading of rights by explicitly giving a user different rights in each subdirectory. For example, you can give a user all rights [ROS] in the SYS:APP directory and the SYS:APP \ DATA \ JSMITH directory. But you can stop access to SYS:APP \ DATA \ GJONES directory by assigning [ ], i.e. null, rights to that directory. Actually, you'll probably find it simplest to give the group EVERYONE [ ] rights to the SYS:APP \ DATA directory and issue rights as needed to users own personal directories.

MAXIMUM DIRECTORY RIGHTS

As LAN manager, you may find it necessary to give certain directories maximum allowed rights. Thus, no matter what rights users have for other directories, maximum rights are restricted for all in those certain directories. In this case, instead of setting EVERYONE group rights with [ ], use the NetWare utility FILER to install the maximum directory rights mask for that directory. When you enter FILER, it presents you a menu such as Fig. 5-5, which shows the current directory at the top of the screen and a list of options. To set the Maximum rights mask, first change to the directory for which you wish to set the rights. If this is not the directory shown at the top of the screen, use the "Change Current Directory" option to change. When at the chosen directory, select Current Directory Information to get to the "Maximum Directory Rights Mask"

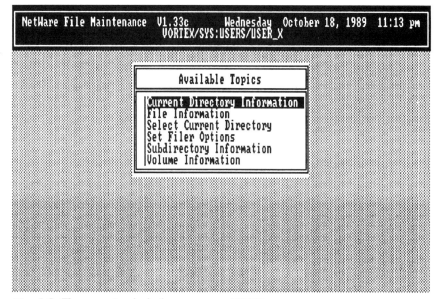

Fig. 5-5. The menu invoked when you enter FILER.

option. After choosing this option, you see a screen similar to Fig. 5-6. The default is all rights. If you decide to limit the rights to a directory, use the Del key to eliminate unwanted rights.

NetWare does a logical AND between the trustee rights and the maximum rights mask to arrive at a user's effective rights to a given directory. Thus, if a user has been granted all rights in a directory, but only [ROS] in the Maximum Rights Mask, that person will only have [ROS] rights in that directory.

GROUPS

Groups categorize users into their respective applications and usage. Although not required, groups can make network management easier and simpler to understand. Sample groups might be Accounting, Management, or Word_Processing. Groups are created with SYSCON in the same fashion as installing users.

To grant rights to a specific directory to multiple users, create a group, assign the rights to the group, then insert into the group all the users who need access. You create groups with SYSCON, but you may assign group rights either with SYSCON or FILER. If a group requires rights to the word processor, you can create a group called WP. Then, assign the WP group rights to access the word processing program.

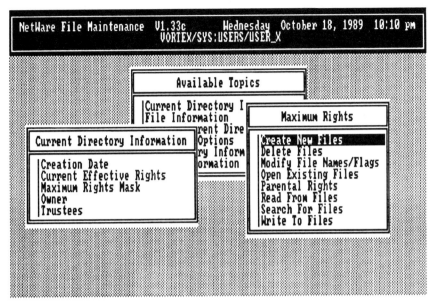

Fig. 5-6. Maximum Rights menu.

FILE SECURITY

NetWare 286 can flag individual files with different rights. You can assign flag files as:

Assignment	Description
Execute Only	Executable files, with extensions of .EXE and .COM only, can be flagged Execute Only so they cannot be copied off of the network. This flag has two caveats. Once a file is flagged Execute Only, you cannot unflag it, only delete it! Also, some programs store overlay files within their executable files. You might get an error if the program tries to read its overlays in the .EXE file after initial loading.
Hidden File	Files flagged as hidden do not show up when you run a DOS directory. However, they do show up when users execute the NetWare NDIR command.
Indexed	If you flag a file as indexed, NetWare indexes the File Allocations Table (FAT) for fast access.

You'll find these Novell FATs sometimes referred to as Turbo FATs. You should index data files with over two to three megabytes for faster access.

Modified Since Last Backup
Backup utilities use this flag to indicate which files have changed since the last time of a backup. NetWare automatically changes this bit when a file is updated.

Read-Only
With this bit flagged, a file cannot be written to or modified.

Shareable
You should flag as shareable, files that are to be accessed by multiple users.

System File
These files belong to the operating system and you should not tamper with them.

Transactional
Flag all files that use Transaction Tracking, as Transactional.

Figure 5-7 shows an example of setting these flags from FILER.

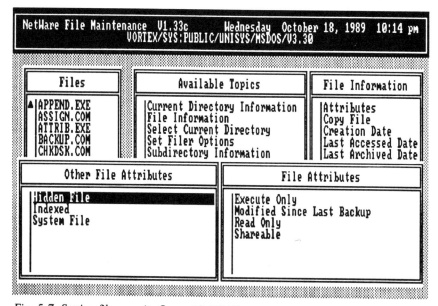

Fig. 5-7. Setting file security flags with FILER.

SUMMARY

NetWare security is perhaps the single feature that has made NetWare the best selling PC network operating system, today. By implementing passwords, log in restrictions, expiration dates, and other user specifications, you can restrict your users from unauthorized accesses. Trustee rights keep sensitive data from other users. You can also protect data from being written over or deleted. File security requires setting flags for specific files that allow protection. NetWare security remains a principle feature of NetWare.

6

NetWare Accounting

LAN resource accounting has become a needed and valued service in many organizations. Accounting allows you to justify the purchase of a LAN and the charges for LAN use. NetWare 2.1 introduced resource accounting to track, limit, and report LAN use. Even if you don't need to charge your users for their time on the LAN, you may be able to use this information for justifying new LAN equipment.

NetWare provides five basic keys for attaching usage charges:

- Connect Time
- Disk Blocks Read
- Disk Blocks Written
- Disk Storage Used
- Service Requests

NetWare allows attaching this usage to a user's account. Novell's software also allows or revokes LAN access according to selected usage levels.

To initialize accounting and set user account balances, use the NetWare utility SYSCON; to monitor and report on usage, use the two supervisor utilities, ATOTAL and PAUDIT.

INSTALLING ACCOUNTING

Accounting actually makes up an internal part of the NetWare operating system. All the accounting programs get installed on the server with the NetWare installation. However, before you can utilize NetWare's LAN accounting, you must initialize it with SYSCON. To do this, log on as supervisor and run SYSCON. The first option SYSCON gives you is "Accounting." When you press the Enter key to select this option, SYSCON asks if you want to install accounting — if it has not been previously installed. If you answer yes, the program initializes values and sets the system flags to enable the account reporting. SYSCON then brings you to the Accounting menu shown in Fig. 6-1. If accounting is already installed, SYSCON immediately displays this menu and bypasses the installation procedure.

Accounting Servers

After accounting has been installed, the first SYSCON choice allows you to modify the authorized servers that are allowed to make charges against a user's account. Normally, only a user's default server is listed. However, other servers, such as those used for printing, mail distribution, and archiving files, may also charge for use.

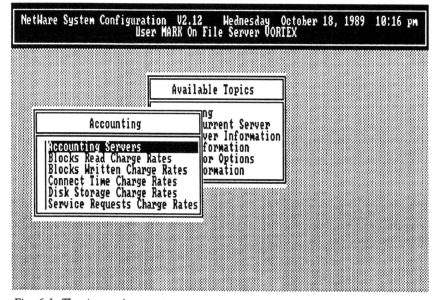

Fig. 6-1. The Accounting menu.

All the other menu choices detail how the user is charged for services. First, let's discuss these charges. Then, you can look at some examples that you might be able to use on your own network.

Charge Rates

The first two charges, "Blocks Read Charge Rate" and "Blocks Written Charge Rate," allow you to charge a user each time he or she reads or writes information to or from a disk. The user gets charged every time, even if they read the same block over and over again. "Units Per Block" provides the rate at which the user is charged. You may define units as any value, for example 1 penny, 1 dollar, or 1/3 dollar.

NOTE: A NetWare version 2.1x disk block uses 4K or 4096 bytes of disk storage space, which is the amount of information NetWare reads or writes at a single time. This value doesn't change, even if you only need to read or write a single byte of information. Novell fixed this amount at 4K for performance reasons.

When you look at the Charge Rate screen, notice the left side. It shows the first charge rate, which defaults to no charge. Also notice that there is "no charge" at all times during the weekend. Figure 6-2 is an example of this screen.

```
╔══════════════════════════════════════════════════════════════════════╗
║ NetWare System Configuration  V2.12   Wednesday  October 18, 1989  10:22 pm ║
║                  User MARK On File Server VORTEX                      ║
╚══════════════════════════════════════════════════════════════════════╝
┌──────────────────────────────────────────────────────────────────────┐
│                                        Sun Mon Tue Wed Thu Fri Sat     │
│        Blocks Read Charge Rates    9:30am  1   3   3   3   3   3   1    │
│                                   10:00am  1   3   3   3   3   3   1    │
│                                   10:30am  1   3   3   3   3   3   1    │
│ Monday                            11:00am  1   3   3   3   3   3   1    │
│ 9:30 am To 9:59 am                11:30am  1   3   3   3   3   3   1    │
│                                   12:00pm  1   3   3   3   3   3   1    │
│ Rate  Charge    Rate  Charge      12:30pm  1   4   4   4   4   5   1    │
│  1   No Charge    11                1:00pm  1   4   4   4   4   5   1    │
│  2   1/2          12                1:30pm  1   4   4   4   4   5   1    │
│  3   2/1          13                2:00pm  1   4   4   4   4   5   1    │
│  4   5/2          14                2:30pm  1   4   4   4   4   5   1    │
│  5   10/1         15                3:00pm  1   4   4   4   4   5   1    │
│  6                16                3:30pm  1   4   4   4   4   5   1    │
│  7                17                4:00pm  1   4   4   4   4   5   1    │
│  8                18                4:30pm  1   4   4   4   4   5   1    │
│  9                19                5:00pm  1   4   4   4   4   5   1    │
│ 10                20                5:30pm  1   2   2   2   2   2   1    │
│      (Charge is per block)          6:00pm  1   2   2   2   2   2   1    │
└──────────────────────────────────────────────────────────────────────┘
```

Fig. 6-2. The Charge Rate screen.

You can change charge rates at half hour intervals. To select a new charge rate, position your cursor over the time to be changed. For multiple times use the F5, MARK, key. When a Select Charge Rate screen appears, it prompts you for a multiplier and divisor to be charged per unit. If you enter a 1 multiplier and a 10 divisor, you charge users 1/10 of a unit every time they access the disk. Then, for every 10 blocks accessed, the user is charged 1 unit. (A unit is defined later in this chapter.)

Connect Time

You can charge users for the amount of time they are logged onto the server, which is the most popular charge rate and the easiest to understand. Connect Time charges operate the same as blocks read/written, except connect time is measured in minutes. Every time a user logs in or out, NetWare records it in the NET$ACCT.DAT file in the SYSTEM directory.

Disk Storage Charges

Disk storage charges accrue for each block a user stores on a disk. You'll find this charge most effective when the "Limit User Disk Space" option is set in NETGEN. When this option is set, the server always keeps a running total of the blocks used by each user. Therefore, at the selected time when charges are to be made, the server already has the totals. Otherwise, the server could be strained while it polls the disk and counts up the total blocks used by each user. However, if charges are to be made at low usage periods, this option might not be necessary.

When you enter a value in "Disk Storage Charge Rates," you designate both the time the server calculates and the charges against the users account for total space used. NetWare uses the rate specified for charging units. Unlike the other accounting charges, the "Disk Storage Charge" charges for all storage in use since the last time charges were made.

Service Requests Charges

You can set up your NetWare LAN to charge every request made of the server. Set up "Service Request Charges" using the same method as block read/write charges. You'll find "Service Request Charges" important when the LAN is used in a service industry that charges clients, by the hour, such as a LAN in an attorney's office. Every time a user talks to the server, he or she gets charged, no matter what the request.

SETTING UP CHARGE RATES

When you first consider setting up your LAN, you'll find no simple way to know how much to charge for each particular type of LAN use. This information depends on why you charge, whether you want to break even or make a profit from these charges, and how users are going to utilize the system. You, as the LAN manager, have to decide the answers to the first two questions. However, the NetWare system utility, ATOTAL, can help with how the system is used.

The best way to do this is to set up your system, initialize accounting, and, then, let it run for a few weeks with normal usage. This approach is used because NetWare does not track usage unless accounting has been initialized. When it has been initialized, NetWare opens a file called NET$ACCT.DAT in the System directory, where it tracks LAN usage. Because NetWare stores accounting data as a binary file, you cannot read it with a text editor, so it is secure information.

ATOTAL

ATOTAL reads the NET$ACCT file in its binary form, interprets it, and displays the information in readable, character form. To use ATOTAL, you must initiate accounting on your server. After your system has run for a while with accounting, you can run ATOTAL and either send your output to your printer or to a file. The output should look like Fig. 6-3. For accurate results, take two or three weeks of usage and average the totals for that time.

DETERMINING VALUES

Let's look at some sample ways to set up accounting. First, assume the values in Fig. 6-3 are your collected sample. You'll use them to average the base for our charges. Second, assume you need to collect $2000 per month from your LAN users to pay for the system. Also, assume you want to collect this strictly for LAN connect time. If you use a four week month, you multiply four times the weekly total connect time to obtain an amount for monthly connect time. In this example, one month connect time totals 86228 minutes. Divide $2000 by 86228 to get a charge of approximately .023 dollars—or 2.3 cents per minute. While this is a good figure for dollar accounting, NetWare wants a fraction with a two-digit number on top and a two-digit number on the bottom. Therefore, round the total minutes to 86000. Now, divide the $2000 by the rounded num-

Fig. 6-3. Example output of ATOTAL.

```
Processing Accounting Records ...


09/04/1989:

      Connect time:      1508      Server requests:     450243

      Blocks read:      32239      Blocks written:       11180


09/05/1989:

      Connect time:      5318      Server requests:    1586676

      Blocks read:      77234      Blocks written:       27952

      Blocks days:          0


09/06/1989:

      Connect time:      1996      Server requests:     344534

      Blocks read:      29794      Blocks written:         713

      Blocks days:          0


09/07/1989:

      Connect time:      9220      Server requests:     454633

      Blocks read:      20978      Blocks written:        1132

      Blocks days:          0


09/08/1989:

      Blocks read:      19466      Blocks written:         895

      Blocks days:          0
```

Totals for week:

Connect time:	21557	Server requests:	3184799
Blocks read:	179691	Blocks written:	41512
Blocks days:	0		

Fig. 6-3 ends.

ber, 2000/86000, which reduces it to 1/43. This is the number you enter into the Connect Time Charge Rate with SYSCON.

The second example charges for Block Reads from the disk. Figure 6-3 shows the total blocks read for the week as 179691. Assume you need to make that same $2000 per one month for blocks read. You can use the same approach as in the previous example.

Multiply the total blocks read times four to get a monthly figure, 718764 for the example. Divide $2000 by 718764 to get .002 dollars per block read as the "Blocks Read charge." Again, NetWare wants a fraction. You could round 718764 to 720000 and reduce the fraction of 2000/72000 to 1/410. However, this gives you dollars per blocks read and you want cents per blocks read. It's actually quite easy to alter the scale to pennies per minute. Because a dollar has 100 pennies, just multiply the numerator of 1 by 100. Now, you are charging 100 pennies per 410 blocks read. Again, reduce it to 10 pennies per 41 blocks read and enter this number into NetWare's Charge back.

PAUDIT

PAUDIT is the second supervisor utility you'll use for LAN accounting. It shows you all accounting transactions that have transpired since accounting was initiated or since the last reset. PAUDIT reads the NET$ACCT.DAT file in the SYS:SYSTEM directory and shows you transaction-by-transaction every login, logout, and charge that has transpired. You can capture this to a file or printer and then delete the NET$ACCT.DAT file to keep this display short. If you let it accumulate for a long period of time with an active system, NET$ACCT.DAT can grow to a very large file.

SETTING USER ACCOUNT BALANCES

SYSCON allows you to set up default values for beginning balances when creating new users. It also lets you alter users' balances on a one-by-one basis. Here we demonstrate both.

Log in to the network as supervisor, type SYSCON, and press Enter. When the Available Topics menu appears, select Supervisor Options to bring up the necessary menu (see Fig. 6-4).

"Default Account Balances/Restrictions" is the first option. Selecting this brings up a list of values to be set (see Fig. 6-4). Most of these values have been explained in the previous chapter on security. The last three values set the default accounting balance for new users.

Account Balance   When you decide to charge for network services, you must decide why you are utilizing accounting. Are you going to allow users unlimited credit and simply track usage for reporting? Or, are you going to charge users and allot them balances in advance? An example of this second process allows users 100 hours of connect time that they pay for in advance or are just given free every month. If you charge 1 unit per minute, you have to set a beginning balance of 6000, 100 hours = 6000 minutes.

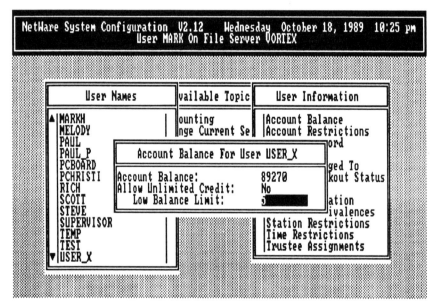

Fig. 6-4. The Account Balance screen accessed by the user supervisor to set or alter user account balances.

Allow Unlimited Credit If you only want to track usage and don't want to deny users access to the LAN because they depleted their balance, you can give them unlimited credit. However, if you charge for the network services and want to get money in advance before a user uses the services you should set this to Yes.

Low Balance Limit When you set a limited credit value, NetWare asks for a low limit that a user may reach before they seek the supervisor to get more credit. This may be a negative limit, if you want to allow them to use the network after their credit has expired.

The best time to set default balances is before users are added to the system. However, because you rarely know the value of the system and charges when installing it, you should wait a few weeks before setting these values. When you set up default account balances, you only affect users set up after charges are established. Therefore, you'll find it necessary to reset all existing user accounts to your default value.

SETTING INDIVIDUAL USER ACCOUNTS

Each user accepts the default balance when it's first created. Take a look at a sample user data. From the SYSCON Main menu, select User Information. From the User Names menu, select a user to examine his or her accounting information. Choose the first option, ACCOUNT BALANCE, and you have the Users Accounting Balance screen similar to that shown before in Fig. 6-4. NetWare shows you the three options— "Account Balance," "Allow Unlimited Credit," and "Low Balance Limit." You can reset these amounts for individual users to customize your system charges.

If you are just tracking usage of your system, you may want to allow everyone unlimited credit and report on usage by the negative amount a user account gets every week/month. To do this, set everyone to a zero balance from the User Information menu. Use the F5, MARK, key and mark all the users you want to reset. When you press the Enter key, NetWare shows you a short menu of all the options you can change for all the selected users. The first one, "Account Balance," is set as described previously and affects all marked users. By entering zero to "Account Balance," all users are set to zero units.

SUMMARY

This chapter explains NetWare accounting functions and how to initiate them. NetWare accounting allows you to track and/or charge for network services. The five accounting services that can be tracked are Connect Time, Disk Blocks Read, Disk Blocks Written, Disk Storage Used, and Service Requests. NetWare's supervisor utilities, ATOTAL and PAUDIT, report LAN activity. You can set default and individual user account balances. Because you can use NetWare's accounting functions many different ways, you'll find the best way is to experiment and try different methods to see which way is best for your LAN.

Login Scripts
and Related Commands

A Login Script is a set of commands that is executed automatically by Novell each time a user logs into the system. As an analogy, you could consider the function of the Login Script as a LAN AUTOEXEC.BAT file. The purpose of the Login Script is to provide a custom environment for the LAN users. There are two types of Login Scripts that are provided by Novell. The first is the *System Login Script* which is executed every time, by everyone. The second is the user-specific *User Login Script*. Every user can have their own custom Login script to set up a working environment that is germane to their own needs, preferences and uses. Figure 7-1 gives an example of a login script screen.

The Login Script is nothing more than a set of commands that is executed by the *Script Language Interpreter*. Like any language, there are variables, control structures, conditionals, and command verbs. Normally, the Novell Login Script is edited and maintained using the SYSCON menu utility, however, this file is really nothing more than an ASCII text file called NET$LOG.DAT in the PUBLIC directory on the SYS: Volume. You may use any ASCII editor to maintain this file if you wish.

DEFAULT LOGIN SCRIPT

Novell comes with a default Login Script. This script is created at installation and looks something like the following:

```
WRITE "Good %GREETING_TIME, %LOGIN_NAME."
MAP DISPLAY OFF
MAP ERRORS OFF
Remark:Set 1st drive to most appropriate directory.
MAP *1: = SYS:; *1: = SYS:%LOGIN_NAME
IF "%1" = "SUPERVISOR" THEN MAP *1: = SYS:SYSTEM
Remark:Set search drives (S2 machine-OS dependent)
MAP S1: = SYS:PUBLIC; S2: = S1:%MACHINE/%OS/OS_VERSION
Remark Now display all the current drive settings
MAP DISPLAY ON
MAP
```

We can use this default login script to cover the basic properties of a login script.

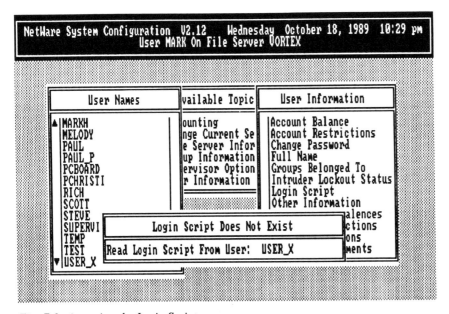

Fig. 7-1. Accessing the Login Script.

The first thing to notice is the use of verbs in the script language. The verbs in this example include WRITE and MAP. WRITE. As their names imply, they write a message to the user's screen. Using the variables GREETING_TIME and LOGIN_NAME, line 1 of the Login Script would print something like "Good Morning, Paul " or "Good Evening, Supervisor" on the workstation screen. MAP is a more complex verb that has a number of uses. Notice lines 2 and 3 of the script. Here MAP is used to turn the display off and suppress error reporting, respectively. The

MAP command also can be used in a fashion very similar to its use as a command line utility to set up logical drive mappings. First, to define drive mapping, use the form MAP X: = SYS: where X is any valid drive letter. Finally, MAP can be used by itself to display the current drive mappings. This is how it is used in the last line of the login script.

The script language also has a set of *system variables*, which can be used to great advantage. These variables include in our above example, GREETING_TIME and LOGIN_NAME. Novell maintains a table of values for these system variables. For example, if the system time is prior to noon, the value for GREETING_TIME will be "Morning" and if after noon it will be "Afternoon." The variable LOGIN_NAME is taken from the login process.

There are also a set of special variables. These *special variables* have values that depend on the current status of the system. Notice the use of *1 in line 5. This variable means "the first network drive." Thus, in a normal network configuration, Drives A: thru E: are reserved for local drives. The first network drive, therefore, becomes **F:**. If, on the other hand, the DOS CONFIG.SYS file contains the line LASTDRIVE = H, then the first network drive would be **I:**. Using *1 ensures that the first network drive will be the target directory, regardless of the DOS configuration of the particular workstation.

Another special variable is S. **S** is a search variable. S1, S2, S3 etc. correspond to the first three search paths maintained by NetWare. A special form of the variable S* means assign the search path to the next available search mapping letter. Again, this gives maximum flexibility in complex Login Scripts.

The script language also implements the IF...THEN control structure for conditional processing. An example of this capability is shown in line 6. If the LOGIN_NAME is Supervisor, you want to make the "home" directory SYSTEM. To do this simply check the value of the LOGIN_NAME and if it is Supervisor, MAP the home directory to SYS:SYSTEM.

The Login Script Language is fairly rich and offers a great deal of flexibility in system control and customization. Let's take a closer look at the rest of the variables and verbs that are available in this language.

LOGIN SCRIPT VARIABLES

Login Script variables called *Identifier Variables* by Novell, can be used with the WRITE command, IF...THEN structures, and commands like COMSPEC, where it is possible to specify a pathname.

Command	*Description*
HOUR	Hour of the day or night (1-12)
HOUR24	Hour in 24 hour format (1-24)
MINUTE	Minute value of the current time (00-59)
SECOND	Second value of the current time (00-59)
AM_PM	AM or PM
MONTH	Number of the current month
MONTH_NAME	Name of month, i.e., January, February
DAY	Day number of the current date (1-31)
NDAY_OF_WEEK	Weekday Number (1-7 with Sunday as 1)
YEAR	Year in 4-digit format (1989, 2015)
SHORT_YEAR	Year in 2-digit format (89, 15)
DAY_OF_WEEK	Text day of week (Monday, Tuesday,)
LOGIN_NAME	Users login name
FULL_NAME	Users full name (assigned in SYSCON)
STATION	Workstation number (first login is 1, etc.)
P_STATION	Actual physical station number, 12-digit hex number
GREETING_TIME	Morning, Afternoon or Evening
NEW_MAIL	Yes or No
OS	Workstation's OS, i.e., PC/DOS, MS/DOS
OS_VERSION	Version number of DOS, i.e., 3.0, 3.1, 3.3, 3.03
MACHINE	The machine that the shell was written for
SMACHINE	Short Machine Name, i.e., ACER, IBM, AST
ERROR_LEVEL	A value where 0 = no errors, x = error number

If you are using any of the above variables with the WRITE Command be sure to precede the variable name with a %.

LOGIN SCRIPT COMMAND VERBS

The following command verbs can be used in login scripts. Typical or usual uses of the commands are shown here, although there may be others. See the Novell Supervisor Reference Manual for the full language definition and additional examples.

ATTACH
ATTACH [*file server*[/*username*[;*password*]]]

Attach is used to provide an attachment to another file server on the network. It is normally used in setting up an environment where there is a primary and secondary file server. If used by itself, the user will be prompted for Server Name, Login Name and Password, just as if entered from the DOS command line. The parameters can also be included to automate an attachment. An example might be the following:

ATTACH MAIL/MAILUSER;MAIL

This login script entry attaches the user MAILUSER to the MAIL server and issues the password MAIL.

BREAK ON/BREAK OFF

Much like the DOS batch file command, the BREAK ON command allows users to break out of their batch files by hitting the Ctrl-Break keys or Ctrl-C. If you do not want users to be able to stop the execution of the login script, issue the command BREAK OFF. The default is OFF.

COMSPEC
COMSPEC = *N[/] *filename* or
drive:[\ ]*filename* or S*N*:[\ ]*filename*

This command works very much like the DOS SET COMSPEC command. In fact, the result of using this command changes the environmental COMSPEC as indicated. The COMSPEC variable points to the location where the COMMAND processor should be loaded from when needed.

COMSPEC = A:COMMAND.COM
COMSPEC = S2:COMMAND.COM

The first example loads COMMAND.COM from the A: drive. The second example causes COMMAND.COM to be loaded from the second drive in the search path.

DISPLAY
DISPLAY [*directory/*] *filename*

FDISPLAY
FDISPLAY [*directory/*] *filename*

This command displays the contents of the specified file to the workstation screen. There are two forms, the first form takes the file as is and presents it on the screen, while the second form performs a filtering operation (hence FDISPLAY) on the file to remove printing characters, word processing control characters and other non-ASCII characters. There are a couple of important uses for this function. It makes it possible to manually or automatically update the contents of a file and have the file automatically displayed each time users log into the system. Suppose the supervisor wants to display a piece of news each day to his users. A file called NEWS could be used to accomplish this task. In a banking environment, you might want to provide an automatic display of current daily interest rates.

DOS BREAK ON/DOS BREAK OFF

This command allows the system manager to control whether the DOS BREAK variable is on or off. If set to ON, then pressing Ctrl-Break or Ctrl-C will cause an application to exit abnormally (if it is not internally trapping keystrokes). If it is set to OFF, then it will prevent breaking out of applications improperly.

DOS SET
DOS SET *name* = *"value"*

This command lets you set a DOS environmental variable from within the login script. The *DOS environment* is a special place where global system variables are stored. Type SET at a DOS prompt to see the current environment. You will likely see at least three variables: PATH, COMSPEC and PROMPT, and perhaps many more. Many DOS applications use the environment to control parameters within their applications. For example:

```
DOS SET PROMPT = "$P$G"
DOS SET USER = "%LOGIN_NAME"
```

The first example sets the DOS prompt to the pathname followed by a "`>`" character. The second sets the environmental variable USER to the NetWare login name.

DOS VERIFY ON/DOS VERIFY OFF

This login script command is identical to the DOS VERIFY command. With VERIFY set to ON, files that are copied using the DOS COPY command will be verified for correctness of the copy.

DRIVE
DRIVE X:
DRIVE *n

This will change the logged drive to the drive specified in the command. Notice that the form *n (where n is a valid drive number) will change to the network drive indicated by the number. If you have four network drives defined as F:, G:, H: and I:, the command DRIVE 3* would change the logged drive to H:.

EXIT

The EXIT command is used to terminate execution of the login script at that point in the login script. The command is recommended where you have long involved scripts, and want to provide a convenient exit point for special circumstances. If, for example, you want the supervisor to be able to exit without multiple drive mappings, menus or other "user" types of settings, you might use a login script entry like:

```
IF LOGIN_NAME = "SUPERVISOR" THEN BEGIN
    EXIT
END
```

EXIT *"filename"* This form of the EXIT command provides an exit from the Login Script and executes the specified program. Valid files to exit to are the executable files, i.e., .EXE, .COM and .BAT. These three examples

```
EXIT "MENU MAIN"
EXIT "DBASE APP"
EXIT "MYBATCH"
```

illustrate exiting to a Novell Menu system, a dBASE application titled APP, and a batch file titled MYBATCH.BAT, respectively.

NOTE: Do not use EXIT to exit to a TSR (Terminate and Stay Resident) program like SideKick, terminal emulator or other such program. If you must execute a TSR program automatically, use EXIT to run a batch file and place the loading of the TSR in the batch file.

#
[directory] filename parameter line

This command (#) executes a command from within the login script. It is treated as though the command were entered from the DOS command line. For example, if you wanted to execute a program from within a Login Script and continue executing the login script, but only when a LOGIN command line parameter is entered, you might use something like this:

```
IF %2 = "PROG" THEN BEGIN
    #PROG
END
```

If a login command like LOGIN PAUL PROG is used, then the program PROG is executed. Keep in mind that over 70K of RAM is used by the LOGIN process (which starts the login script running). Therefore, you have that overhead, in addition to the DOS overhead and the network shell overhead.

FIRE PHASERS
FIRE PHASERS x TIMES

Novell has included a rather unique noise generator in its script language. Fire Phasers makes a noise like a "phaser" gun from a science fiction movie. Many system administrators use this as an alert signal on their networks.

```
WRITE "Set up for %USER_NAME"
FIRE PHASERS 4 TIMES
```

This example might be used as the last line in a Login Script to indicate that the system has been set up for a particular user and note that fact with the firing of the "phasers."

IF/THEN
IF *conditional*(s) THEN *command*

The IF...THEN statement in the Login Script provides most of the power of the language. You can have the Login Script test for a variety of conditions and only take a course of action based on the conditions. The conditional can use the variables that are discussed above. Some examples of valid IF statements should be helpful:

```
IF DAY_OF_WEEK = "Friday"
IF GREETING_TIME IS NOT "Morning"
IF MEMBER OF "GROUPNAME"
IF %2 = "PROG"
```

There are two forms to the IF...THEN condition statement. The first is a *single line* implementation. The action and the evaluation of the condition are on the same line. For example:

```
If DAY_OF_WEEK = "Friday" then WRITE "Today is Payday!"
If MONTH = "2" AND DAY = "29" THEN WRITE "IT MUST BE
    LEAP YEAR"
```

If you need to execute *multiple command lines* based on the conditional, then use the form IF...THEN BEGIN ... END. An example should make the form clear:

```
IF LOGIN_NAME = "PAUL" THEN BEGIN
    REM Set up drive mappings
    map g: = vortex/sys: \
    map h: = vortex/sys:util
    map i: = vortex/vol1: \
    map j: = vortex/vol2: \
    map k: = vortex/vol3: \
    map l: = vax/sys: \
    map m: = class/sys: \
    map n: = class/vol1: \
    REM Set up environmental variables
    DOS SET USR = "PCHRISTI"
    DOS SET PWD = "MACROBIND"
    DOS SET S_USER = "%FULL_NAME"
    REM Set up a default capture
    #CAPTURE q = printq_1 nt nb nff ti = 10
    REM Exit to my menu system
    EXIT "Menu Paul"
END
```

In addition to the variables that you can use, there are a complete set of relationship operators. The equality operators are summarized here:

Equality	*Inequality*
Is	Is not
=	! =
= =	< >
Equals	Does not equal/Not equal to

In addition there are other relational operators:

Operator	*Description*
>	Is greater than
<	Is less than
> =	Is greater than or equal to
< =	Is less than or equal to

One major limitation of the script language in its present form is the ability to nest IF...THEN statements.

INCLUDE
INCLUDE [*directory* \ ]*filename*

The INCLUDE command is designed to facilitate the inclusion of script command lines that are external to the script contained in NET$LOG.DAT. With extremely long Login Scripts, it is nice to have a full blown text editor available for editing. Another use of this command is a convenient way to test and update a complex login script. The INCLUDE command can be nested up to 10 levels deep, which means that an INCLUDE in the main login script can call a file with an INCLUDE statement which can call another and so on up to 10 levels.

    INCLUDE sys: \ cmdfile

In this example, the file cmdfile is included in the login script as though it were a part of the main file.

MACHINE
MACHINE NAME = *"machinename"*
MACHINE = *"machinename"*

This is another command with two forms. The purpose of this command is to set the machine name variable to the name given. Some DOS programs need this variable in order to run properly.

MAP

MAP is a command with many forms. Its primary form has to do with managing disk drive mappings. Those forms include the following:

MAP   Displays the current drive mappings for all defined drives.

MAP *drive*   Displays the current mapping for the drive specified.

MAP *drive*: = *directory*   Maps the designated drive to the directory indicated, for example, MAP X: = SYS:TEST.

MAP *drive*: = *drive*:   Maps the first drive to the same directory that is being pointed to by the second drive.

MAP INSERT *search drive*: = *directory*   This command will insert a search drive using the next available drive designation.

MAP DEL *drive*:   This form of the MAP command will remove the drive designated from the map definition table. For example, if Drive X: is defined as SYS: \ PUBLIC \ UTIL then MAP DEL X: removes this definition. Now when you type MAP at the DOS prompt there is no reference to Drive X:.

MAP REM *drive*:   Exactly the same as MAP DEL.

In addition to its use with managing drive mappings MAP can be used for handling the display and errors:

MAP DISPLAY On/Off   With the display mapped on, drive mappings will be displayed when logging in. Conversely, with it mapped off, drive mappings will not be displayed. The default is ON.

MAP ERRORS On/Off   With errors mapped off, error messages will not be displayed. Conversely, with it mapped on, errors will be displayed. The default is ON.

PAUSE/WAIT

Like the DOS batch command file PAUSE, this command pauses in the execution of the Login Script and prompts the user to "hit any key to continue."

REMARK

REMARK causes all remaining text on the same line to be ignored. This is very helpful for commenting the Login Script. It is also a convenient way to eliminate executing certain lines of the login script when you do not want to permanently remove the lines. NOTE: Equivalent forms of the same command are **REM**, *, or ;.

WRITE

As you have seen in the default login script and the examples above, the WRITE command is used to send information to the screen during the login process. There are some special characters that can be used in the WRITE command. These include \r for a carriage return, \n for a newline, \ " for an embedded quote. All text must be enclosed in double quotation marks.

The System Login Script is an extremely important part of setting up a smooth running Novell network. It enables the custom configuration of the overall user environment to make as secure, comfortable and user friendly system as possible. The System Login Script is the script file that is run for everyone. However, each user can also have a User Login Script. This login script is executed when the System Login Script is completed.

USER LOGIN SCRIPT

The User Login Script is created from the SYSCON utility. Select User Information, followed by the User Name. One of the items on the User Information menu is Login Script. Simply enter the appropriate Login Script Language commands for the user.

Novell provides a very nice feature with the User Login Script. If there is no script in existence when you select it, you will be given the opportunity to copy a script from another user. Obviously if you have many user scripts that only differ from each other slightly, this can save a lot of typing.

The user's Login Script is located in the user's MAIL directory. To find this file, locate the user's ID number from SYSCON. It is on the User Information menu item labeled Other Information. This is a six-character id. Change to the Mail Directory and then to the user's directory. The file name is LOGIN and like the System Login Script, it is a plain text file.

Configuration File Options

Special configuration information for each user relating to their shell can be placed in a special file called SHELL.CFG. The file should exist in the same directory as the IPX.COM and NETx.COM. Some of the options that can be placed in the SHELL.CFG file are used by IPX and others are used by NET3. Like most of the other files used by Novell, this is a plain ASCII text file. A sample SHELL.CFG file might look something like the following:

```
SHORT MACHINE TYPE = COMPAQ
LONG MACHINE TYPE = CMPQ
READ ONLY COMPATIBILITY = ON
LOCAL PRINTERS = 0
SEARCH MODE = 3
IPX SOCKETS = 15
FILE HANDLES = 50
```

IPX Options

IPX SOCKETS = *n*   This option changes the maximum number of sockets that IPX can have open on a workstation and does not need to be changed except for very unusual applications. The default is 20.

IPX RETRY COUNT = *x*   This option tailors the number of times that a workstation should resend a packet. The default is 20.

SPX CONNECTIONS = *x*   This option changes the number of SPX connections that can be used at the same time from that workstation. The default is 15.

SPX ABORT TIMEOUT = *x*   This adjusts the amount of time that SPX will wait without receiving a response from a connection before it terminates the connections. The default is 540 (30 sec.).

SPX VERIFY TIMEOUT = *x*   This option adjusts the frequency at which SPX sends a packet to inform the other side of the connection that it is still active. The default is 540 (30 sec.).

SPX LISTEN TIMEOUT = *x*   This option adjusts the amount of time that can pass without receiving a packet before sending a packet to request whether the other side is still active. The default is 108 (6 sec.).

IPATCH = *x, y*   This option allows the patching of the IPX.COM file. The *x* value is the byte offset and the *y* value is the value.

It should be obvious that these configuration options are extremely advanced and should only be used when required by the application or in very unusual circumstances.

NETx SHELL File Options

The SHELL.CFG options that affect NET2 or NET3 are shown here:

CACHE BUFFERS = *x*   This option determines how many cache buffers are to be used for caching nonshared, nontransaction tracking files. The default is 5.

FILE HANDLES = *x*   This option adjusts the number of file handles a workstation can have open at a time. The default is 40. Some applications require more than the default number of files.

PRINT HEADER = *x*   This option changes the size of the buffer that is used to hold printer setup sequences before a print job. The default is 64 bytes.

PRINT TAIL = *x*   Like the print header option, this option sets the size of the buffer that is used to hold the setup sequences (escape codes) that are used after a print job to reset the printer. The default is 16 bytes.

EOJ = *On/Off*   Use this option to change the automatic closing of files, locks, semaphores etc., at the end of a job. The default is ON.

HOLD = *On/Off*   Use this option to determine whether files should be held open by the workstation until the application program exists. The default is OFF.

SHARE On/Off   This option determines whether a child process will inherit the same file handle of the parent process, or a copy. The default is ON.

LONG MACHINE TYPE = *name*   This sets the MACHINE variable, which can be used by the Login Script. It is normally used to help set the correct search path to the DOS version used on the machine. The default is IBM_PC.

SHORT MACHINE TYPE = *name* This option sets the SMACHINE variable for use with the Login Script. The default is IBM. As an example, setting the value to CMPQ enables the use of the CMPQ$RUN.OVL file for use with menus and other utilities. This is limited to 4 characters.

LOCK RETRIES = *x* This will control the number of retries attempted to get a lock on the LAN. The default is 3.

LOCK DELAY = *x* This will control the amount of time that the shell should wait before executing a retry to get a lock. The default is 1.

READ-ONLY COMPATIBILITY = *On/Off* There is a difference in the way NetWare 2.0 and NetWare 2.1 handle Read-Only files. This is used to make NetWare 2.1 look like 2.0 for applications that are not aware of the difference.

LOCAL PRINTERS = *x* This option sets the number of local printers attached to the workstation. The importance of this option is primarily in workstations with no printers attached. If you inadvertently hit the Shift-PrtSc key, this option can prevent the workstation from hanging, if capturing is not implemented.

SEARCH MODE = *x* This option lets you change the way that the shell searches for a file not in the currently logged directory. The default is 1 and the Modes are listed below:

- *Mode 1* If a path leading to the data file is specified in the executable file itself, search only that path. If a path is not specified, search the default directory and all search drives.

- *Mode 2* Search only the currently logged directory.

- *Mode 3* If a path leading to the data file is specified in the executable file itself, search only that path. If a path is not specified and the executable file opens data files Read-Only, search the default directory and then all search drives.

- *Mode 5* Search the default directory and all search drives.

- *Mode 7* If the executable file opens data files Read-Only, search the default directory and all search drives whether or not the path is specified in the executable file.

- *Mode 0* No search mode specified. Look for instructions in the workstations boot diskette in the SHELL.CFG file.

MAXIMUM TASKS $= x$ This option controls the number of tasks that can be active at any one time. The default is 31 and the Range is 8 through 50.

PATCH $= x, y,$ This option allows the shell to be patched with any value. The x variable equals byte offset and the y variable equals the value.

TASK MODE $= x$ This option allows compatibility with Windows 386. If set to 1, the shell will check for Windows 386 virtual tasks and if set to 0, it will not check for Windows 386 virtual tasks.

NETBIOS File Options

There are a variety of NETBIOS options available. For purposes of this chapter, we simply list the options available; please check the Novell manual if you need further information.

- NETBIOS SESSIONS $= x$
- NETBIOS SEND BUFFERS $= x$
- NETBIOS RECEIVE BUFFERS $= x$
- NETBIOS RETRY DELAY $= x$
- NETBIOS ABORT TIMEOUT $= x$
- NETBIOS VERIFY TIMEOUT $= x$
- NETBIOS LISTEN TIMEOUT $= x$
- NPATCH $= x,y$

SUMMARY

Novell has provided the NetWare user and system administrator with a wealth of capabilities to custom tailor a system. Users as a whole and the individual user should have few problems meeting whatever operational requirements exist. Most users will not need to deviate very far from the default configuration, or implement exotic Login Scripts to handle their requirements. However, it is always comforting to know that if you need to make a change you most likely will have the capability at your fingertips.

PART III

Printing

Printer Installation and Capturing

NOVELL NetWare offers great flexibility for printing from a network. However, as a result of that flexibility, NetWare users also suffer many hours of confusion and aggravation when trying to print. With NetWare, you have access to multiple printers—some may be located next to your desk and some may be in the next building. With this extended printer-access capability, you don't have absolute control over every printer since many users may share each network printer. On the up side, you probably have access to faster and better quality printers than might be available to an individual.

This chapter guides you through the printing process. It explains the various printer handling utilities that are provided with NetWare. After reading this, it is hoped you will be less confused, less aggravated, and on your way to being a NetWare printing expert.

NETWORK PRINTING

A single-user PC directs all printed information to the local printer connected directly to the computer. In a network environment, you can still print data locally or you can redirect printed output to the NetWare file server, where it gets captured into a queue until the printer is ready to print. This second process is called *spooling*. If the network printer is ready, it prints the data as soon as the server receives it. If this printer is currently printing another job or is unavailable for other reasons, your job stays in the queue until the printer finishes and is ready to print your information.

PRINT QUEUES

NetWare print queues manage all printer information passed to the network. Whenever printed by a network printer, data must first pass through a *print queue*, which is a holding area that can receive multiple print jobs and print them one at a time, while still receiving more information. At the time of installation, NetWare creates a subdirectory for each queue under the system directory. NetWare gives the directory a name associated with an identification number assigned the queue at its creation. This directory serves as a holding area for spooled information until the printer is ready. NetWare gives each separate job its own file in this directory.

By managing printers in this fashion, NetWare allows you to designate multiple printers to service a single print queue, which allows print jobs to be printed at a much faster rate. NetWare also allows a single printer to service multiple queues, which you'll find useful when you want one queue to have a higher priority than another. This allows important print jobs to be placed in front of other jobs already in the queue.

DEFAULT QUEUES

NetWare assigns a default queue for each printer defined during installation. Default queue names differ only by the number of the queue. Queue names take the form of PRINTQ_#, where # is the number of the network printer. If printer #1 is defined on the server, its corresponding default print queue name is PRINTQ_1. These defaults allow users to begin printing immediately without initially defining alternate print queues.

NOVELL PRINTER UTILITIES

Novell provides several utilities to manage the network printing and the network print queues:

Program	*Function*
CAPTURE	Redirects a local workstation printer port to the network printer

ENDCAP	Ends the redirection of CAPTURE
NPRINT	Prints an existing file to a network printer
PCONSOLE	Manages network printers and print queues
PRINTDEF	Defines printer codes and forms
PRINTCON	Defines specific print jobs for applications
PSTAT	Shows the current status of the network print queues

Users employ CAPTURE, ENDCAP, and NPRINT to send output to the network printer. PCONSOLE, PRINTDEF, PRINTCON and PSTAT primarily manage the network printers and are discussed in the next chapter.

The CAPTURE Command

The CAPTURE command redirects to the network printers data sent to workstation's local LPT ports. Workstations don't need to have these ports installed to redirect them. CAPTURE will simulate one or all three ports to allow redirection to different printers and/or files at the same time.

Some applications written for use with NetWare directly access the network printers. With these applications, you can use network printers without issuing a CAPTURE command. However, most plain DOS applications do not directly address the network printers. These applications send data to local printer ports in a stand-alone PC. Use CAPTURE to enable such "non-NetWare-aware" applications to send data from the workstation to a network printer or to a network file.

When you execute CAPTURE, you can specify several flags that indicate where and how the information is to be printed. Flags are the same for both CAPTURE and NPRINT, although not all of them are available to NPRINT. If you type CAPTURE and don't give any flags, the program supplies the default flags as follows:

CAPTURE SERVER = (default file server) QUEUE = printq_0
PRINTER = 0 LOCAL = 1 FORM = 0 COPIES = 1 TIMEOUT = 0
BANNER = LPT1: NAME = (username) TABS = 8 FORMFEED
    AUTOENDCAP

The CAPTURE flags (you can also use the short form shown in brackets) are:

SHOW [SH]   Displays the current settings of all network printer redirection. All ports show, along with where they print, what flags were issued during capture and if output is also stored in a file. Don't use with any others.

TIMEOUT = *n* [TI]   Provides a method to print the contents of the queue job without exiting the application. The default value of 0 does not let the information print until you exit your application. Because most programs will not close the printer port when finished, CAPTURE lets you specify a certain amount of seconds it can remain inactive before it closes the current queue job. Then, it reopens another queue job and continues sending data to the printer. The *n* number can be 0 through 1,000.

HINT: Most single user and non-network applications find the default timeout value of 0 insufficient. Most application programs need a *timeout value* to begin printing and will not print until you exit. (We've found that a timeout of 10-15 seconds usually works.) If the value is too large, you have a while to wait for printing. If the value is too small, you might print half a report before it's done, which can happen if the application stops to calculate some values while printing.

AUTOENDCAP [A]   An alternate to the Timeout feature. Use this option to close the print job to the queue upon exiting the application. The default, AUTOENDCAP is on. Because most programs require a timeout to work satisfactorily, you will use this function primarily to reverse a NOAUTOENDCAP flag.

NOAUTOENDCAP [NA]   Use this flag if you are printing from several applications and want a single printout at the end of the session. It forces the queue to wait for an ENDCAP before printing the information.

LOCAL = *n* [L]   NetWare can spool all three local printer ports at once. By replacing *n* with 1, 2, or 3, you can designate which port you are currently flagging to capture.

SERVER = *name* [S]   Specifies the job to go to a printer attached to another server. If you are not logged onto the specified server, it logs you on as GUEST. If there is no GUEST account, or there is a password assigned to the GUEST account, or if GUEST does not have rights to the specified print, you will have to supply login information in order to print.

JOB = *name* **[J]**   This can be specified if it has been previously defined through PRINTCON. You can define a job to have flags preset, which can set multiple flags by specifying one job name.

PRINTER = *n* **[P]**   Network printers can be numbered 0 through 4, which are set at the time of installation. If you wish to print to a specific printer, then designate its printer number here.

QUEUE = *name* **[Q]**   The queue name can be a default set up by the system such as PRINTQ_0 or it can be one you have created with PCON-SOLE.

FORM = *name* or *n* **[F]**   Indicates the type of paper currently in the printer. You can also address forms using numbers or by a form name if you have created one with PRINTDEF.

COPIES = *n* **[C]**   Prints multiple copies from one print job, to a maximum of 255. When 0 is used in conjunction with the create flag, the output is captured to a file for later editing or use.

CREATE = *name* **[CR]**   Prints data into a file so it can be edited or input into another application. With CREATE, you specify a file name to be created to hold all of the printed information.

TABS = *n* **[T]**   A few programs print a control code instead of a specific number of spaces for a tab. If the application does not format the tabs into spaces for you, use the spooler to delete the tab control characters and insert the specified number of spaces. The flag accepts values between 0 and 18.

NOTABS [NT]   Some printers require the control characters passed through untouched, which not only holds true for tabs, but also for other characters that might be significant to the printer. Postscript printers and other special units sometimes need this flag to properly print from the network.

HINT: TABS = 8 is the default configuration for capture. If you are printing graphics output you will want to issue a NO TABS statement.

NAME = *name* [NAM]   Specifies the name to appear on the top of the banner page. The banner page, the first page to be printed, lists information about the job printing. The page defaults to the name of the current logged-in user, which is very helpful if many people use the same printer.

BANNER = *name* [B]   Specifies the name to appear on the bottom of the banner page and can be up to 12 characters long. BANNER usually describes the information being printed. The default is LST:.

NOBANNER [NB]   For small print jobs or where the printer does not receive heavy use, NOBANNER can save paper, because no banner page is printed.

FORMFEED [FF]   Some programs do not advance printer paper to the top of the next page after printing, which can be hazardous because the next person might print on the following line of the same page you just finished. Send FORMFEED to the printer following the completion of a print job to avoid such over-printing.

HINT: Most word processors send a formfeed after the last page is printed. Spreadsheets, screen prints, and most other programs will need this feature set to ON.

NOFORMFEED [NFF]   Stops the network from sending a formfeed to the printer. If the application sends a formfeed after the document, turn off the FORMFEED function.

KEEP [K]   A safety feature, stores all print information at the server and, if a workstation fails, it prints all the information that it has received thus far. If you plan to capture data over an extended period of time or have problems with a workstation, use this option. If this option is not used, server discards the information if the computer fails.

The ENDCAP Command

The companion program to CAPTURE, closes one or more capture ports from the local workstation to the network. To end a capture session from one or more of a workstation's LPT ports, use ENDCAP. As with CAPTURE, use flags to indicate which port you are controlling. By default, ENDCAP stops only the first LPT port. If you wish to control others, include one or more of the following flags:

LOCAL = *n* [L]   Ends CAPTURE for the local port specified, which can be 1, 2, or 3.

ALL   Ends all capture sessions for all LPT ports.

CANCEL [C]   Stops the current session and also discards the contents of the print job from the print queue. Nothing gets printed with the network printer. For example, CANCEL LOCAL = 2 cancels the capture session from workstation LPT port 2, while CANCEL ALL cancels all network printing currently in progress on all ports. These, like all CANCEL commands, discard the data that has already been sent to the queue.

USING CAPTURE AND ENDCAP

The CAPTURE command should be part of the menu and program batch files. If you don't have a local printer, you'll find it useful to specify LOCAL PRINTER = 0 in the workstation SHELL.CFG. Thus, in case no CAPTURE command is active, the workstation will timeout faster and not try to access your local ports. Some examples of capture follow. We have used the short form for our examples to get you familiar with using them. Refer to the previous definitions for full descriptions of the commands.

The Show Flag   To see current status of the LPT ports, enter the following command:

CAPTURE SH

If no capture command has been issued, CAPTURE displays:

LPT1: Capturing Is Not Currently Active.
LPT2: Capturing Is Not Currently Active.
LPT3: Capturing Is Not Currently Active.

If you issue CAPTURE without any flags and show the current configuration again (CAPTURE SH), it displays:

LPT1: Capturing data to server COUNT
    Capture Defaults:Enabled Automatic Endcap:Enabled
      Banner   :LST: Form Feed :Yes
      Copies   :1   Tabs:Converted to 8 spaces
      Form   :0   Timeout Count :Disabled

LPT2: Capturing Is Not Currently Active.
LPT3: Capturing Is Not Currently Active.

The current settings can be displayed at any time on the network.

Examples

To CAPTURE all information to the first network printer as sent from an application to a local workstation LPT:, enter at the DOS prompt:

CAPTURE TI = 2

Then, run the application. Now, all the information that normally prints to your local workstation printer port is redirected to the network printer. Here we are using a short timeout value of two seconds indicated with the TI = 2. To resume printing locally, exit the application and enter:

ENDCAP

This closes the CAPTURE session to the server and stops the redirection.

The following command redirects LPT3 to network printer #2. The NO BANNER flag eliminates a banner printing before the print job. Programs such as WordStar send a formfeed at the end of the print job, thus the NO FORM FEED FLAG. The information will also print if nothing is sent to the printer for 5 seconds.

CAPTURE L = 3 p = 2 nb nff ti = 5

SAVING DATA TO A FILE

Use the CREATE command to generate a network file to hold all information sent to the queue. When using CREATE, also use the NOAU-TOENDCAP flag to ensure that the server doesn't close and reopen the file you are spooling to, which would cause the already saved data to be overwritten. Use the command:

CAPTURE CR = FILENAME.TXT NA

Then, after all the information has been captured, issue an ENDCAP command to close the file. Once the file has been closed, you can edit it or save it for future printing.

NPRINT

Use NPRINT to print existing files on the network. You can directly send text files, captured files, and other files to print queues. NPRINT uses many of the same flags as CAPTURE, with one addition: **DELETE** allows you to automatically delete a file after printing it. Of the flags listed for CAPTURE, NPRINT does not use flags like Create, Show, Timeout and Autoendcap.

Using NPRINT

To print a file with NPRINT, give the command followed by the file name and any flags, if they differ from the defaults. The defaults remain the system defaults, unless you set up a default print job through PRINT-DEF. For example, if you want to print the file REPORT.DOC located in the public directory, type:

```
NPRINT F:\PUBLIC\REPORT.DOC
```

If you want to print the file on network printer #2 and no banner is necessary, use the command with the appropriate flags:

```
NPRINT F:\PUBLIC\REPORT.DOC p=2 nb
```

SUMMARY

In this chapter, you have learned how to use the basic programs to send data to the network printers:

- The CAPTURE command sends your print job to the network printers.

- The ENDCAP command stops the CAPTURE sending or printing to a local printer.

- The NPRINT command sends an existing file to the printer.

You also have learned the parameters that can be used along with these commands to customize and adapt your printout.

9

Printer & Queue Management

NETWARE uses three programs to define the printing process and control it—PRINTDEF, PRINTCON, and PCONSOLE. You don't have to utilize these programs to begin printing. However, if you use them and properly define the printer setups, then the three programs can enhance your network and make it easier for all to print. As a network administrator, you can use PRINTDEF to define print devices and to specify print modes available from these devices. Using PRINTCON, you can configure and create the job names for the users to call when accessing these modes. The user can instruct the network to use a specific print job configuration from CAPTURE, NPRINT, or PCONSOLE. Finally, PCONSOLE lets you see what is currently printing and add print jobs.

PRINTDEF

PRINTDEF defines printers, output devices, and print forms used throughout your network. With PRINTDEF, you define the type of device and the print codes necessary for controlling and operating that device. You can configure functions such as reset, draft mode, and different fonts. Then, you can send them to the printer automatically, depending on your network's configuration. You can also set up forms, such as Letterhead and Green Bar, so that the printer defaults to the correct print size and margin for those specific forms. However, you must have supervisor rights to modify the information in PRINTDEF.

DEFINING PRINT DEVICES WITH PRINTDEF

Of course, print devices vary for each network. Print devices, as defined by Novell, are network objects, such as printers and plotters. You'll encounter two basic steps when you define a print device with PRINTDEF: 1) First, you must define the functions the device has available. These functions consist of escape sequences that instruct the device to perform the specific functions built into it. 2) Second, you must define print modes for that printer. *Modes* consist of one to several predefined print functions that are used by PRINTCON.

SETTING UP PRINT FUNCTIONS

Print functions can take time to set up. Novell's NetWare includes several common print device definitions, such as Hewlett-Packard Laserjets, Epson printers, and others. If your printer is one of the included ones, you'll save hours of work. Otherwise, you'll have to refer to your printer manual for the codes required to implement its various functions and fonts. With these codes available at hand, you can begin your printer definition.

First, you must log onto the LAN as supervisor or with supervisor equivalent rights. After login, access the PRINTDEF utility by running it in the public directory. PRINTDEF displays the opening menu shown in Fig. 9-1.

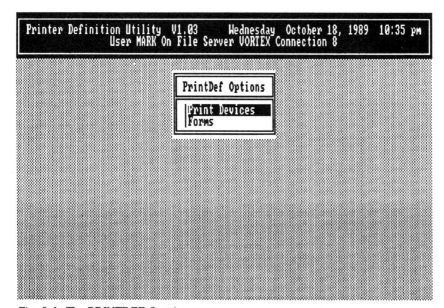

Fig. 9-1. The PRINTDEF Opening menu.

Use the Return key to select Print Devices. PRINTDEF gives you the options to edit a current device, import an existing printer definition file (PDF), or export an existing definition to a PDF to be transferred or saved for backup.

If the NetWare supplied drivers were loaded during your NetWare installation, select IMPORT. Choose the SYS:PUBLIC directory for the source directory when prompted. (If, after selecting this option, no devices appear, you have to copy them onto your file server.) PRINTDEF presents you with the list of available PDFs for common network print devices. Press the Down Arrow until your PDF is highlighted and select it by pressing the Enter key. If your print device is not listed, you will have to create a PDF for it, which is discussed later in this chapter.

After selecting the device to import, PRINTDEF returns you to the print device option menu. If the program prompts you for a device name instead of returning you to the menu, you already have a device defined by that name. In that case, either type in a new name or press the Esc key to cancel. Now, let's look at the imported printer definition. Select EDIT PRINT DEVICE to see a list of the printer definitions currently in the PRINTDEF database. If this is your first import, only one is listed. Select it by pressing the Enter key.

The program displays a menu that lets you edit either the device modes or the device functions. To NetWare, a *device mode* is a group of device functions needed to achieve a specific output. Some functions might include print style, size, and boldness. For example, most printers require a command set called ''re-initialize'' that resets it to its default state, usually what's available just after you turn it on. This re-initialize command can be as simple as a single character or it can be as complex as a series of characters that require an entire line for the definition.

To look at the available printer functions, press the Down Arrow key and select DEVICE FUNCTIONS, which gives you a list of currently defined functions and their corresponding escape codes. All these functions together make up the device mode. You can also assemble a combination of any of these to make up your own device modes.

Installing a New Print Device

If, after looking through the defined print devices, you don't find your specific device, you need to create one. Use the PRINTDEF menu and select EDIT PRINT DEVICE, which displays the Defined Print Devices list. Press the Ins key to insert your new device. Then, the program prompts you for a new device name. Use a name that can be recognized by all network users. For example, ''HP Laserjet'' is preferable to ''Laser Printer'' because you might later install a different brand of laser printer.

After you name the device, you need to define its print functions. Select Edit Print Options followed by the Functions Menu. This brings up a blank list because no functions are currently defined. You have to rely on your printer documentation for a list of all the codes that control it. Usually, you'll find a separate chapter that describes in detail your printer's control codes and an appendix that summarizes them.

To enter a control code, press the Ins key, then enter the function name and its corresponding control code sequence. Name each definition to describe its specific purpose. A common example resets the HP Laserjet printer. Enter RESET as the function name. After pressing the Enter key, move down to the control code definition. HP Laserjet documentation tells you the reset string is "Escape e". PRINTDEF uses the Esc key to indicate the infamous Escape character (ASCII 27), as used not only by H-P printers, but also by most other brands of printers. Enter other control code characters just as they appear. For the Laserjet example, enter Esc-e and press the Enter key. Press the Esc key followed by the Enter key to save your new function and to insert it into the Functions list.

We used the example of the commonly found HP Laserjet Reset sequence. However, every device should have a reset sequence that returns it to default mode. Because network printers get used by many people who print many different ways, Reset is a very important function that should be entered for all printing devices. If somebody prints a spreadsheet sideways and does not reset the printer, the next person who uses the printer will have their report printed sideways. We recommend that you use Reset as the first command for all your printer functions. If you need to edit any of your defined functions, select them by positioning the cursor over them and pressing the Enter key. After editing them, press the Esc key and save them as before.

IMPORTING FROM ATTACHED FILE SERVER

If the PDF file you need is located in another file server that you can presently access, use the Backspace key to erase the displayed directory path. Press the Ins key for a list of attached file servers and highlight the file server you want to import from. Press the Enter key to implement your choice.

If the PDF file is located in a file server you cannot presently access, press the Ins key twice. The software displays a list of "Other File Servers." Highlight the server that contains the PDF file you wish to copy and then press the Enter key. A box appears asking for your login name and password. Fill in the proper entries. After you log in, you'll get a list of the volumes available on the source file server. Select the volume with your file and press the Enter key. Another list appears that displays the available directories in the chosen volume. Select the one you want and press Enter. After you complete the directory path entry, press the Esc key, then the Enter key. The software prompts for the PDF file you want to import. Select the file and NetWare automatically imports it. Finally, the file name gets inserted into the defined device list for your server.

DEFINING DEVICE MODES

After defining the functions for a print device, you can combine them into modes. A *mode* contains a sequence of print functions that tells the printer how to print a particular job. For example, your print modes might include Draft, Final, and Sideways Condensed. While each one has specific uses and can be used individually, you can also let NetWare take care of printer control, which makes network management a little easier.

After entering PRINTDEF, select the PRINT DEVICE. From the list of print devices, select the one you want to view or edit. Choose DEVICE MODES to get a list of the various modes that have been defined. If this is a new device, only the Reset mode is available. To view or enter the re-initialization functions for your printer, highlight Re-initialize and press the Enter key. NetWare displays any current strings that are sent to the printer for initialization. If this is a new device, nothing appears. In this case, press the Insert key to define a new mode. The software presents you with a list of the current functions currently defined for the device. Use the cursor keys to select a ''reset'' function and press the Enter key. You can use the F5 key, the "Mark" key, to select multiple functions that may be needed to accomplish the printer's reset. Use the steps detailed above to insert any modes that can be useful to your network users.

SAVING THE PRINTDEF DATABASE

After defining your print functions and modes, you have to save the changes. Press the Esc key until you come to the Exit Printdef menu. Respond Yes and the menu shown in Fig. 9-2 appears. Choose Save Data Base to make your changes permanent. NetWare leaves you at the DOS prompt ready to proceed to the next step, defining forms.

DEFINING FORMS

Print forms, defined by NetWare, specifies the type of paper used for printing by network users. The print forms you define set up print job

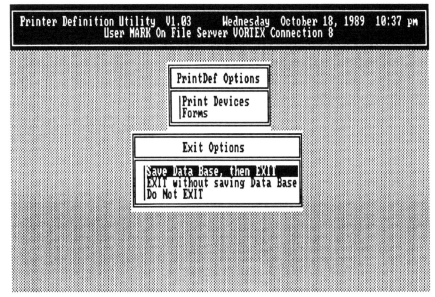

Fig. 9-2. Saving the PRINTDEF database.

configurations. Print forms can be as simple as plain white paper or as ornate as letterhead. Print forms let the server know which paper is currently loaded in the printer.

The file server uses a form name and number. *Form definitions* contain a form's name, number, the number of lines per page, and the number of characters per line. Figure 9-3 is an example of the entry screen. When you send a print request that requires a specific form, the file server will not print the job until that form is mounted in the printer.

Let's define a standard form. Enter PRINTDEF and select the FORMS option. PRINTDEF displays the current list of defined forms. If no forms have been defined, none are listed. Press the Ins key to insert a new definition. The Form Definition screen displays. Enter the name STANDARD for the form name and press the Enter key, which moves you to the form number box. Numbers can be used instead of the form name to mount a form. You can have up to 255 forms defined per server. Type a 1 and press the Enter key to define form number 1. Next, NetWare asks for the number of lines per page to be printed. While forms can have from 1 to 255 lines per page, a standard page usually has 60 or 66 lines. Enter 60 and press the Enter key. The last piece of information needed, the number of characters per line, can be between 1 and 999. A standard $8^1/_2$ × 11-inch piece of paper with 10 characters per printed inch has 80 characters per line. Enter 80 and press the Esc key to exit. Then, NetWare asks whether you want to save the information. Select "Yes" to save or "No" to release the definitions just created.

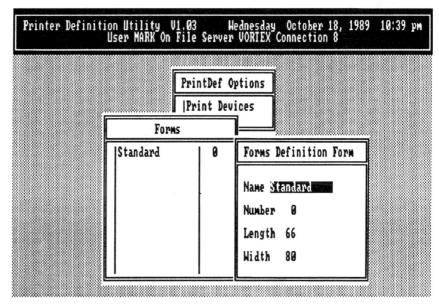

Fig. 9-3. The Form Definition screen.

You edit and change forms in a similar way. When the list of current defined forms is displayed, select the one you wish to edit. NetWare gives you the same screen as when defining a new form, except the current form definition is already there. Edit the fields as necessary and press the Esc key to save any changes.

Deleting forms is similar to inserting them. Position the cursor over the form to be deleted and press the Del key. NetWare asks you to confirm the deletion of the form. To carry it out, select Yes and you are returned to the forms menu.

PCONSOLE: NETWORK PRINT CENTRAL

Novell provides NetWare with a master program for controlling all general printing options. PCONSOLE, the network printing console, is a menu-driven utility that helps you set up and control printing needs. Network users can access PCONSOLE as a utility to insert, modify, and delete their own print jobs, or as a print queue utility to control the jobs in a particular queue. Network administrators can use PCONSOLE to set up and modify the queues and their operating environments.

USING PCONSOLE

Run PCONSOLE to get the menu shown in Fig. 9-4. "Change Current File Server" allows you to examine and print with printers and

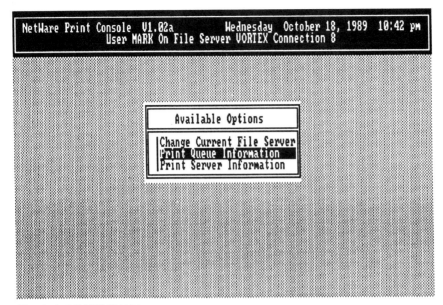

Fig. 9-4. PCONSOLE Main menu.

queues on other file servers. "Print Queue Information" provides the general queue management option. "Print Server Information" displays all known print servers and their print server information.

Print Queue Information

When you select "Print Queue Information," PCONSOLE displays all the currently defined print queues. When you set up the default printers during NetWare installation, you assigned each one a default queue. NetWare assigns queues with the names of PRINTQ_0, PRINTQ_1, PRINTQ_2, PRINTQ_3, and PRINTQ_4, depending on the number of printers you defined with NETGEN. When you send a print job to printer 1, NetWare places it into PRINTQ_1 for subsequent printing.

Now, let's select a queue to examine. Because PRINTQ_0 is the first to be defined, choose it. PCONSOLE displays the menu shown in Fig. 9-5.

Current Print Job Entries

Selecting "Current Print Job Entries" allows you to see the current print jobs in the queue. If you have the proper rights, "Current Print Job Entries" allows you to modify the current print jobs in the queue. It also allows network users to submit print and delete their own jobs by pressing

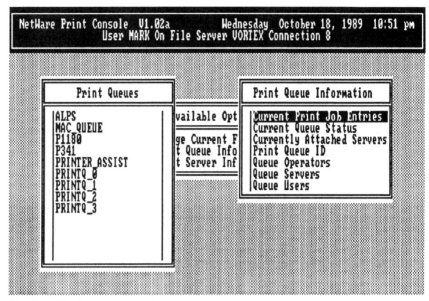

Fig. 9-5. The Print Queue Information Users menu.

the Insert key or the Delete key. If the queue has any entries waiting to be printed, they are listed on the screen in the order received by the queue.

Each line lists a single entry into the queue. The first piece of information PCONSOLE tells you about each entry, the "service sequence," is the order in which the jobs will be printed. Second, each entry shows you the banner name of the job. If the user specified "no banner to be printed," PCONSOLE substitutes the user's (or client's) name for reference. Next, PCONSOLE displays a description of the print job. Most application software does not currently utilize this feature. The only times you might see this information are when you redirect the local printer port with CAPTURE, or if you actually submit the job through PCONSOLE and supply a description. In these cases, you see the name of the local port redirected or the user description of the job. The form number used for the print job follows the description. NetWare defaults to form 0.

Next, PCONSOLE displays the current status of the job. There are four status types—active, ready, waiting, and held. A job currently being serviced by a printer is considered *active*. Even if the printer is offline, PCONSOLE still considers a job active because the computer constantly tries to print it and holds the job active. A job marked *ready* is ready to be printed but has not had a printer available to service it. Most jobs follow through the ready to active cycle as they are printed. A job flagged as *waiting* has been submitted with a specific time and date for printing, maybe because large print jobs can best be run in the middle of the night when demand for the printer is low. The last flag, *held*, allows users who have rights to the specific print job to place a hold on it. If the printer malfunctions, you might need to place a hold on the job until the printer is repaired.

The final job flag displayed on the Print Queue Information Users menu, "Print job ID number," is an incrementing number that tracks all print jobs that have passed through the queue since the server was turned on.

Print Queue Entry Information

If you select a job, the current parameters of that job are displayed, which is a complete listing of all the specifications for the job. The information should look like Fig. 9-6.

Most of these flags under the CAPTURE command are described in Chapter 7. You can change any of the flags from what was chosen at the time the job was submitted. You also see a few flags that can't be changed because they were set by a third party program or directly manipulated by PCONSOLE. These are the *user* and *operator hold*, the *sequence number*, and the option to *defer printing* until a later time and date. The time and date a job was inserted into the print queue is also displayed, but cannot be altered.

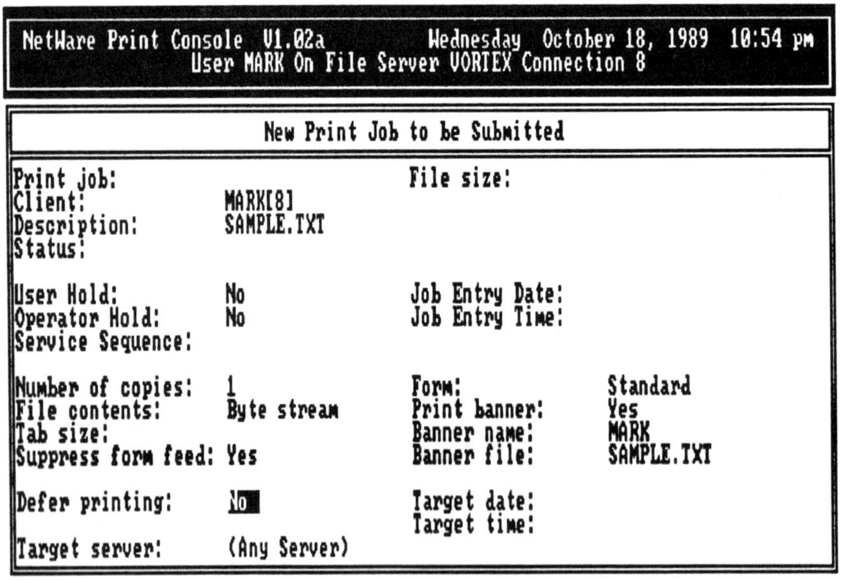

```
┌─────────────────────────────────────────────────────────────────────┐
│ NetWare Print Console  V1.02a          Wednesday  October 18, 1989  10:54 pm │
│                  User MARK On File Server VORTEX Connection 8          │
└─────────────────────────────────────────────────────────────────────┘

┌─────────────────────────────────────────────────────────────────────┐
│                   New Print Job to be Submitted                       │
├─────────────────────────────────────────────────────────────────────┤
│ Print job:                    File size:                              │
│ Client:            MARK[8]                                            │
│ Description:       SAMPLE.TXT                                         │
│ Status:                                                              │
│                                                                      │
│ User Hold:         No          Job Entry Date:                        │
│ Operator Hold:     No          Job Entry Time:                        │
│ Service Sequence:                                                     │
│                                                                      │
│ Number of copies:  1           Form:            Standard              │
│ File contents:     Byte stream Print banner:    Yes                   │
│ Tab size:                      Banner name:     MARK                  │
│ Suppress form feed: Yes        Banner file:     SAMPLE.TXT            │
│                                                                      │
│ Defer printing:    No          Target date:                          │
│                                Target time:                          │
│ Target server:     (Any Server)                                      │
└─────────────────────────────────────────────────────────────────────┘
```

Fig. 9-6. The Print Queue Entry Information screen.

By changing the sequence number, you can move a print job up in priority in the queue to be printed faster. At this point, you can also specify for a job to be deferred. If you defer the job, PCONSOLE prompts you for the time and date you want the job printed.

Print Queue Status

CURRENT QUEUE STATUS allows network users to view the status. Network administrators can change the status flags of the queue. The number of jobs currently in the queue and the number of servers servicing the queue is displayed. Three operator flags also are displayed for allowing new jobs to be placed into the queue, the currently attached servers to service the queue, and to allow new servers to be attached to the queue.

PCONSOLE: WORKING WITH PRINT QUEUES
(Supervisor Options with PCONSOLE)

As the network administrator working with PCONSOLE you have specific responsibilities:

- Creating print queues

- Appointing queue users

- Appointing queue operators or managers

- Setting up print servers

However, all of these responsibilities are optional. NetWare sets up default values for these responsibilities at the time of installation. Manual control over these options just allows NetWare to be more flexible when needed.

Creating Print Queues

NetWare's default installation of the network operating system automatically assigns a print queue to each printer port found in the system. When the file server is first initialized, the system automatically links the NetWare created queue with its respective printer. This automated installation system works for a one-to-one correspondence between printer and queue. However, NetWare allows you the flexibility to have multiple printers serviced by one queue and multiple queues to service one printer.

Multiple printers serviced by one queue ensures faster printing of jobs. Multiple queues servicing one printer allows a specific print job to

be put in front of other jobs going to the same printer, because one
queue's priority is higher than another's.

If you are going to use either of the preceding NetWare print queue
features, you not only have to create the queue (if necessary), but you also
have to instruct the server spooler that it is already done.

You'll find that creating a print queue is a relatively easy task. First,
enter PCONSOLE while logged in as supervisor or with supervisor
equivalent rights. To do this, be sure you've either changed to the public
directory or that you have a search path set to the SYS:PUBLIC directory.
Then, type pconsole and press the Enter key. The menu shown in Fig. 9-
7 is displayed.

Highlight Print Queue Information and press the Enter key. PCON-
SOLE displays the currently defined "Print Queues" that were created at
the time the system was installed. As with all NetWare utilities, simply
press the Insert key and you are prompted for a "New Print Queue
Name." Give the queue a name that describes the service it will perform
or the printer it will service. Good examples might be "Invoices" or
"LASERJET." Enter the name of your new queue now. Your new Queue
name is now displayed in the Print Queue list.

NOTE: If you try to put a space in your Queue name, PCON-
SOLE replaces it with an underline (_).

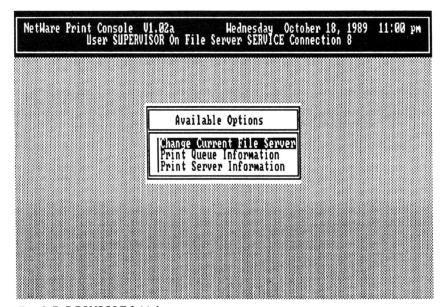

Fig. 9-7. PCONSOLE Initial menu.

Remember, creating a new print queue does not accomplish anything unless you assign it to a printer with the spooler command. You must either assign the queue name to a printer at the console or through the AUTOEXEC.SYS section of SYSCON. See those sections for the correct usage.

You can also rename and delete print queues with a similar process. To delete a print queue, simply highlight the queue name from the "Print Queues" list and press the Del key. NetWare prompts you for confirmation of the deletion. If you select "Yes," the queue name gets deleted from the list, but not from any Print Jobs that may use it as defined with PRINTCON. If you do delete a queue that was used in a defined print job, you should also delete such a print job.

To rename a print queue, go to the "Print Queues" list and highlight the queue name to be changed. Use the NetWare Modify Key, if your computer supports this function. For most computers, it's the F3 key. To check this, press the F1 key twice, so NetWare gives you a list of available keys. If you check with NetWare's help system for a key list, press the Esc key to return to the "Print Queues" list. Press the F3 key and a box is displayed with the current queue name. Use the Backspace key to delete the name and enter the new name. Press the Enter key to save the new name.

Assigning Queue Users

When you create a queue using PCONSOLE, you must also specify which users can place print jobs in the queue by inserting them into the Queue User list. When the queue is created, the group EVERYONE is automatically assigned as queue user. If you wish to limit the users that can use the queue, you need to delete the group EVERYONE and insert your queue users.

The process to insert queue users is similar to creating the queue. After running PCONSOLE, select Print Queue Information at the Available Options menu. A list of the currently defined queues is displayed. Select the queue you wish to change. Select Queue Users at the bottom of the list and the current list of user names that are able to utilize this queue is displayed, as shown in Fig. 9-8.

As with all NetWare menu utilities, the Ins, Del, and Enter keys let you add, delete, and select new users to add to this list. After selecting all queue users, press the Esc key to return to the Print Queue Information menu.

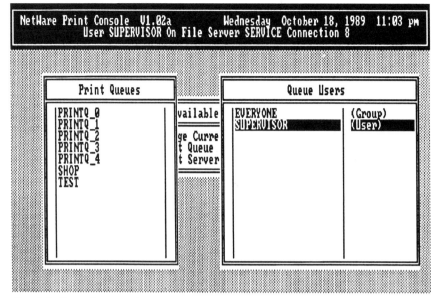

Fig. 9-8. Print Queue Information screen in PCONSOLE.

Queue Operators

Notice there is a menu option to assign "Print Queue Operators." A *queue operator* has the rights and responsibilities to manage the print queue. That person can insert and delete queue jobs and edit parameters for a job waiting to be printed.

To assign your queue operators, select Queue Operators and the current list of operators displays. Insert queue operators just as you did queue users. Use the Insert key and then select the users or groups to be operators. Operators can also be deleted with the Del key.

INSTALLING PRINT SERVERS

The NetWare server may have up to five printers directly connected, which can be up to three parallel printers and two serial ones. NetWare can act as a print server to these five ports. Sometimes, if you have a large installation, you'll find it more convenient to place printers in several departments. If you need more than five printers or if logistics don't allow for convenient server/printer installation, a print server can be an asset.

Because setting up a print server requires third party software, we cannot adequately describe the process here. Most third party print server software usually has its own installation program, some of which create the queues and print server without PCONSOLE. If you decide on a third party print server, refer to the documentation for the package you are installing.

SUMMARY

NetWare's ability to control print devices can be greatly enhanced by using the utilities PRINTDEF, PRINTCON and PCONSOLE. Print devices can be defined through PRINTDEF. Print modes and functions can be defined through PRINTCON. PCONSOLE can be used to make inquiries of the print queues and define print servers throughout the network. Although these utilities are not required for operation of your print devices, using them can make your network more flexible and capable for the end user.

PART IV

Electronic Mail and Productivity Enhancement Software

10

Work Group Software

UNLESS the users on your LAN need some of the more advanced electronic mail (E-Mail) services offered, for example DaVinci Mail, you may want to consider installing a "groupware" program instead of just plain E-Mail software. What's *groupware*? It's software that helps integrate your LAN work group into a more cohesive unit. All the groupware programs that we know of have an E-Mail module. Of course, each groupware manufacturer sees different solutions to the problem of helping networked users work together.

In addition to E-Mail, the five groupware packages we look at in this chapter at least offer *in-common individual user calendaring* and *group event scheduling*. While EMail lets your work group communicate, this other common groupware function lets LAN users avoid conflicts when group members schedule both individual appointments and group activities.

In this chapter, we look at five groupware packages, the most popular ones available as we write this book. They are, in alphabetical manufacturer order: **The Coordinator II** from Action Technologies, **Higgins** from Conetics Systems, **Office Works** from Data Access Corporation, **Right Hand Man** from FutureSoft, and **WordPerfect Office** from WordPerfect Corporation.

CHOOSING A GROUPWARE PACKAGE

When you choose software for individual use, you have the liberty of selecting a program that fits the user's level of expertise, for example, an integrated "point and shoot" menu system for a novice user or command-line speed for a "power" user. However, when you choose software for use with a LAN, particularly something like a groupware package that gets used by everybody, you've got to target the least experienced user. Therefore, groupware should have an easy-to-use user interface that anybody can learn quickly.

Four of the five packages in this review have menu-driven interfaces. The fifth, WordPerfect Office, uses the WordPerfect interface, which, because of the popularity of that word processor, has become a standard in its own right. While easy to learn for people who use other WordPerfect Corporation products, learning WordPerfect Office may prove to be a bit of a challenge for those who don't know that interface system. Of the other four, The Coordinator II and Office Works use standard variations of the "bounce bar" menu system popularized by Lotus 1-2-3. Higgins and Right Hand Man also use variations of the 1-2-3-type interface, but those adaptations are somewhat non-standard. Therefore, we believe users who are familiar with other software that uses the 1-2-3 interface may take longer to adjust to Higgins and Right Hand Man, as we did.

Calendaring, the feature common to all five groupware packages probably provides the primary reason for choosing one of these packages over plain E-Mail software. In fact, in our experience, calendaring may prove even more valuable to your LAN work group than electronic mail, particularly if it saves valuable employee time by avoiding schedule conflicts. All the calendar functions provided by these five software packages were acceptable, but some fill certain group needs better than others. You may want to give calendaring more weight than other factors when choosing a groupware package, particularly if your work group has scheduling problems.

Higgins shows a calendar with five weeks and indicates the current day's schedule with a bar graph. The calendar tracks both appointments and a "to-do" list of items. Office Works group scheduling, while not as straightforward as Higgins, allows more flexibility because you can search for specific items in descriptions attached to scheduled events. WordPerfect Office not only offers scheduling of individuals and groups, but also of resources, such as an overhead projector. The calendaring functions of these three packages are about equal in power and offer the most full-featured calendaring for both personal and group scheduling.

The Coordinator II's calendaring, one of its simpler features, is integrated into its messaging system. The program displays a six week calendar that lets you choose any set of days for appointments. When displaying your appointment, this software also references any messages you have indexed to that appointment. We found The Coordinator II very useful in preparing for meetings. Right Hand Man has the weakest calendaring powers of the five packages. But, if your work group doesn't have heavy scheduling needs, it may do the job.

These five programs all provide adequate E-Mail power for most work groups. They let you send and receive messages, set up private and public mailing lists, forward and reply to mail, CC (carbon copy) mail to yourself and others (except Right Hand Man), and attach files to E-Mail messages. All except Office Works have a Terminate and Stay Resident (TSR) utility that lets you know if you have E-Mail waiting when you're working with other software.

Now, let's look at each package in alphabetical manufacturer order.

THE COORDINATOR II

With a conversation management concept at its core, The Coordinator II provides a highly structured environment for work group planning and message exchange. Action Technologies structured their software around the proposition that work is based on active conversations. To implement this conversation approach, the company created a standard set of openings and responses for communicating with others, also allowing you to integrate conversations with your calendar for individual planning. All this adds up to a powerful package that, with some training and adjustment by users, can be an effective group work management tool. While The Coordinator II can only really manage individual calendars, the company's public relations literature indicates that group scheduling will be added soon—probably by the time this roundup is printed.

The Coordinator II comes with two manuals—written poorly enough so we found ourselves re-reading things several times to figure out meanings. We also found a few errors and a couple of commands that are not listed in the index.

The Coordinator II differs from the earlier version, which many users criticized for its user interface. With this release, Action Technologies has done a great deal of work on the interface, providing a much more intuitive command structure, while giving increased flexibility. The new interface follows the IBM Systems Application Architecture/Common User Access (SAA/CUA).

When The Coordinator II first runs, the opening screen is clear except for a status line across the bottom and a command line on top. You access commands using the Alt-letter keystroke combination that corresponds to the highlighted letter of the command you want to implement. As an alternative, you can hit F10 to access the command line, which allows Lotus 1-2-3 style bounce bar command selection. At any time, F1 brings up context-sensitive help. The Coordinator II offers two levels of menu choices—novice and advanced. Depending on the menu choice and the user level selected, menu choices may pull down sub-menu windows that allow more selections. With its new menu system, we found the program very easy to learn and use.

The Coordinator II Main menu gives you: *Read, Compose, Calendar, Organize, File, Edit, Tools, Exit,* and *Help.* "Read," "Compose," and "Organize" work on messages, and "Calendar" on personal scheduling, the rest on text and file manipulation. Figure 10-1 shows the opening menu options when accessing the calendar. You do most of The Coordinator II activity by reading and responding to messages. You can use "Organize" to review a certain group of messages by type (promises, requests, open matters, etc.), date (by date of communication), category of conversation, or just all the communications with a specific person. We found this approach very helpful when we'd accumulated a large number of messages.

Action Technology bases the structure of The Coordinator II on a few intelligent propositions:

- Work group productivity is carried out through people talking (communicating) with each other.

- Tasks get accomplished through the course of conversations.

- Most conversations start out with one of the seven defined types of purpose.

- Most conversations are directed towards a conclusion.

Action Technologies designed The Coordinator II to implement these simple propositions, forming a structure that, when learned and used, should improve the productivity of your work group.

When composing conversations, The Coordinator II gives you either one or seven choices, depending on user level. If you've selected the novice menu, you can only use the Note form of message. If you turn novice mode off, you can access the seven defined conversation types: *Note, Inform, Question, Offer, Request, Promise,* and *What If* as shown in Fig. 10-2. The novice menu allows the beginner to start communicating right away, while still providing the structured communication that is the basis for The Coordinator II.

Read   Compose   **Calendar**   Organize   File   Edit   Tools   Exit   Help

```
┌ Show calendar... ──────────┐
│                            │
│  From  Wed 18-Oct-89       │
│  Thru                      │
│  ────────────────────────  │
│  October, 1989             │
│  Sun Mon Tue Wed Thu Fri Sat│
│    1   2   3   4   5   6   7│
│    8   9  10  11  12  13  14│
│   15  16  17  18  19  20  21│
│   22  23  24  25  26  27  28│
│   29  30  31   1   2   3   4│
│    5   6   7   8   9  10  11│
└────────────────────────────┘
```

Enter Esc=Cancel F1=Help   Fri 20-Oct 4 06pm

Fig. 10-1. The calendar option accessed from the Main menu of Coordinator II.

Read   **Compose**   Calendar   Organize   File   Edit   Tools   Exit   Help

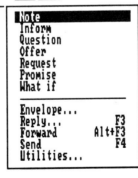

```
┌────────────────────────┐
│ Note                   │
│ Inform                 │
│ Question               │
│ Offer                  │
│ Request                │
│ Promise                │
│ What if                │
│ ────────────────────── │
│ Envelope...            │
│ Reply...          F3   │
│ Forward       Alt+F3   │
│ Send              F4   │
│ Utilities...           │
└────────────────────────┘
```

Enter Esc=Cancel F1=Help F10=Actions   Fri 20-Oct 4 04pm

Fig. 10-2. The Coordinator II's message writing menu.

We found the close integration of calendar and message base in The Coordinator II to be a real plus. Although it is not as rich in features as other software, the calendar does provide enough functionality for day to day usage. When receiving dated requests from others, the program automatically updates your calendar to remind you of pending tasks.

We found The Coordinator II message editor simple and easy to use. For example, to edit and save messages and simple text files, you access the File menu with the Alt-F key combination. The program uses standard ASCII format, so files can be used with other word processors. When choosing a file, you can type in the name or select it by highlighting the file name. The Coordinator II word processor uses modified Word-Star-type editing keys; you can also access the same editing functions using the Editing menu accessed with the Alt-E combination.

One feature of The Coordinator II we found very handy, the built-in windowing system, which lets you work on multiple program tasks open at the same time. For example, you can have your calendar and current messages on the screen and move back and forth between the two.

The Coordinator II comes with and uses a separate mail program, Message Handling Service (MHS), developed by Action Technologies and packaged by Novell with copies of Advanced and SFT NetWare, to send and receive messages. Other manufacturers are also accepting MHS as a messaging standard. Ashton-Tate's FrameWork III comes MHS-ready; WordPerfect has stated its products will soon support MHS. The program provides a standard platform for communication within a single LAN, LAN-to-LAN, and to Remote workstations and LANs. You can also get MHS gateways to connect to IBM PROFS and DISOSS, DEC's ALL-IN-1 and VMSmail, Wang Office, HP-DESK, CompuServe's Info-plex, FAX, TELEX, and MCI Mail, which gives The Coordinator II and any other MHS-base messaging system very powerful message handling.

Installing The Coordinator II

The Coordinator II auto-installs, allowing you to choose between a standard or custom installation. Standard installations automatically alter your NetWare system login script, making life easy for novice LAN administrators.

HIGGINS

Higgins, a relatively comprehensive implementation of group productivity software, gives network users a personal to-do task management system, network-based mail, phone message management, and scheduling for both individuals and groups.

Higgins comes with a separate tutorial manual and a sample data set. The documentation includes a 150-page Reference Manual, a 75-page Tutorial Guide, and a 100-page System Administrator manual. We found the documentation clear and well written.

Although Higgins is fairly straightforward and mostly well thought out, the program has some quirks that make it somewhat tricky to use and not very easy to learn. For example, the main menu uses what appears to be a Lotus 1-2-3 type bounce-bar type selection scheme. However, you can't move the menu selection highlight with the cursor keys. Rather, you use the spacebar or Tab key to move forward in menus and the Shift-Tab keystroke combination to move backward. We found it quite disconcerting to remember *not* to use the cursor keys for menu selection, in contrast with so many other software products that use the 1-2-3 type menu selection system.

Another Higgins quirk shows itself when editing a field. If the cursor sits in a highlighted field that you want to edit, you expect to be able to move to the correct position in that field for editing, say, to the right to change a letter. If you make the intuitively obvious move with the right cursor key, instead of the cursor moving right, it moves to another field. You actually have to select the field, then select Modify from the Commands selection menu near the bottom of the screen. The real editing takes place in an un-highlighted location on the bottom line of the screen, not in the highlighted field itself. While the process works, it takes a great deal of adapting, particularly if you are used to a more conventional software interface.

If you choose Higgins, plan on having your work group spend some time readjusting their thinking to Higgins user interface. We found it much like trying to teach a WordStar user to use WordPerfect—suddenly nothing works the way you expect or want.

The mail system forms the heart of the Higgins software and facilitates network communication. Like CC:Mail, Higgins has a large number of accessories available for special E-Mail needs.

The mail system provides the usual capability for sending mail to single or multiple recipients; for copying to one or more people; and for attaching files to messages. The message editor is somewhat basic and uses a modified subset of WordStar keystroke controls. You select message recipients from a bounce bar menu. Message headers include fields for date, time, to, from, subject and CC (copy). It also includes flags for confirming the message, as well as, private, urgent, and action information elements—comments, action, signature, approval, and edit. The urgent flag ensures recipients get messages immediately, but only if they happen to be using Higgins at the time.

The Higgins to-do function tracks personal to-do items in a coordinated logical fashion. You can assign priority to-do items, attach them to a schedule, and manage them by project, due date, or status. The program has convenient commands to add, move, extract, print, order, reschedule, delete and to mark to-do items as they are completed.

Higgins gives you a personal data filing system, which uses a keyword method of access and retrieval. It allows you to enter general information for later retrieval. The Higgins system also has an expense reporting feature. You can attach an expense item to any schedule or log item in the system. Expense tracking includes the usual date, item, category, number, amount, purpose, where, who and what. You can view expense items, edit them and generate a periodic expense report.

Overall, we found Higgins adequate for most installations. However, while it's full-featured and workable, it's also quirky and difficult to adjust to using it.

Installing Higgins

Higgins auto-installs, although the network administrator must create the program's working directory. A separate program Hignew enters new users.

OFFICE WORKS

While Office Works offers mail, telephone messages, document control, personal and group calendaring, and a name and address database, the program differs significantly from all the other software in this roundup. Those other groupware systems were written as programs with assembly language and/or a high-level programming language, such as C or Pascal. Data Access Corporation constructed Office Works as a database application with its DataFlex database management system (DBMS).

The system comes with a special "Run-Time" version of DataFlex, which allows the Office Works application to run, but which won't run other DataFlex applications. However, DataFlex can read Office Manager files. Because the Office Works Run-Time module differs from the standard DataFlex Run-Time module, you'll need both modules on your server if you have any standard DataFlex applications. Also, because it's written as a DBMS application, Office Works appears to run a little slower than the other software in this review.

Office Works comes with well written documentation that provides excellent help. You get four manuals: a quick start pamphlet, installation, administration, and users' guides.

The Office Works Main menu follows the familiar Lotus 1-2-3 bounce-bar pattern. Highlight a command and press the Enter key or just press the first letter of the command. Main menu selections drop down other vertical menus of selections that work just like the Main menu. A "Tutor" choice on the Main menu helps new users quickly get up to speed with Office Works. The F1 key brings up context-sensitive help.

The electronic mail worked well, but its editor is somewhat primitive. While Office Works "Prepare messages" allow transmission via Telex Easylink over a FAX machine, the software really doesn't actually send your messages. You prepare messages for such transmission with Office Works, which exports them to ASCII files. The program then "chains" with batch files to your Telex or FAX software; those programs do the actual transmission work.

You can also archive older messages, which fits in with the Office Works document control system. This system allows you to archive all types of files, with a message about what's in the file. While Office Works document control system works all right, it just doesn't do enough. For example, you must manually enter document information, if that document wasn't prepared with Office Works. You can't just tell the program to read all the files in a directory.

We found Office Works adequate for most installations. It's full-featured, and workable, with an excellent user interface, but somewhat slow.

Installing Office Works

Office Works auto-installs from compressed archive files on four disks. Because of the archival removal process and because of the large number of files (about 130), installation takes considerably longer than expected. Although the Office Works installation procedure is complex, it's totally menu driven and quite easy.

RIGHT HAND MAN

Right Hand Man, more like Borland's SideKick than a full-featured groupware productivity package, provides limited functionality and is probably most appropriate for small networks. The program's Main menu offers the following functions:

- Appointment Scheduler

- Black Book and Dialer

- Calculator

- DOS Commands and Windows
- Editor
- File Manager
- Guarded Notepad
- Index Files and Dialer
- Macro Keys
- To-Do List
- Electronic Mail
- Notepad
- Phone Message Center
- ASCII Chart
- Typewriter
- User Maintenance
- Transfer window
- File Transfer
- Group Scheduler

The Right Hand Man manual is adequate, consisting of four sections totaling about 150 pages, well written, clear and comprehensive. Of note, the manual binder, while attractively decorated is made of flimsy cardboard and is not very functional. When you run Right Hand Man, it remains TSR in memory, allowing you to run other software with it. You activate Right Hand Man by pressing the Ctrl-R keystroke combination twice, which pops up its Main menu in the middle of the screen.

Right Hand Man has some quirks that you'll need to address before using the program. One of its "features," a type-ahead buffer, increases the MS/PC-DOS 10-character buffer to 96. Unfortunately, Right Hand Man comes with the buffer set to ON, which can negatively affect other software and cause some real frustrations. Because of what appears to be some strange kind of internal delay, the type-ahead buffer can make a workstation appear to lock up, when it actually hasn't. With Right Hand Man in memory while using WordStar or WordPerfect, we got as few as three or four characters entered into a document, when the workstation appeared to freeze. Following the normal user reaction to try to make something happen and verify that the machine has indeed locked up, we banged on the keyboard, entering a random group of characters. All of the sudden, the PC unfroze and all the garbage just entered appeared on the screen. Of course, we should have exercised some self-control and just waited for the type-ahead buffer to clear itself, but most users don't work that way.

Another frustrating Right Hand Man "feature," is that the program comes with its loud, obnoxious key-click set to ON. Our advice, the first time you call up Right Hand Man is to use the F5 key to access the configuration menu to turn off the type-ahead buffer and the keyclick. Once entered, such configuration changes become permanent. One Right Hand Man nice touch is that you can set configuration changes for individual users or as global for all users.

Right Hand Man suffers from some of the same quirky design features as Higgins. The menus, although Lotus 1-2-3-like with selected items highlighted, do not function with the cursor keys. You must enter the first letter of the menu item to make your choice. Causing even more frustration because of inconsistencies, the cursor keys move bounce-bar highlights when making non-action choices. For example, in the messaging system, the cursor keys handle the selection of a particular item on a list of messages.

Right Hand Man's work group features include electronic mail, but the implementation is somewhat rudimentary. The program sends and receives mail, can get a receipt verifying mail has been received, and allows you to edit and delete messages. When you are using other software, Right Hand Man will also notify you that a message is waiting. But, while messages can be sent to multiple addressees, the program has no copy (CC) feature. In selecting addressees, the software pops up a window that prompts for users. A bounce-bar menu even gives you a list of users on the system, but you must manually enter the addressee's name. Hitting the Enter key with a user name highlighted doesn't produce the expected message. An interesting feature is that you can use wildcards when entering names. But, how often do you only send messages to people whose names begin with "S" (S*), or who have the letters "OM" in their name (*OM*)?

Right Hand Man's "message waiting" notification has a lag and a quirk. A full five minutes passed after a message was sent before addressees received notices of messages waiting. Later, when no messages were waiting, Right Hand Man kept popping up "EMAIL WAITING."

The other major Right Hand Man groupware feature, a phone message taker, is one of best implemented features of the program. We found it straightforward, clean, and easy to use. The only complaint is that the message screen comes up with the menu item "DEL" highlighted. You have to be careful that you don't hit the Enter key without moving the menu highlight or you'll lose the message.

Among its non-work group features, Right Hand Man comes with a pop-up calculator, notepad, auto dialer, ASCII chart, and a file manager. It also has a protected or guarded notepad, which saves password protected notes in an encrypted format. The file manager allows multiple copies, deletes, and renames, as well as a file view and edit. Simply tag a file and select the group function. Right Hand Man can also sort directories.

For TSR software offering as many features as it does, Right Hand Man is fairly frugal with memory; the program only uses about 64K. Even so, with NetWare's RAM requirements, Right Hand Man might prohibit the running of application software with large memory needs, such as DBMSs. Right Hand Man appears to be a product with a whole lot of potential, but with a rough user interface and some quirky design implementations. We hope it will mature with future releases.

WORDPERFECT OFFICE

WordPerfect Office appears to be based on the manufacturer's Word-Perfect Library. That earlier released software package offers individual users a calculator, a personal appointment calendar, a file manager, a flat-file database manager, a macro editor, a programming editor, and a menu-driven shell that controls access to other software. In addition to network versions of the WordPerfect Library utilities, WordPerfect Office gives you electronic mail and a group scheduler. The Main menu is shown in Fig. 10-3. The folks at WordPerfect Corporation appear to have done a good job using this software to fill in the gaps left by normal application software, particularly for a networked work group.

WordPerfect Office documentation is thorough, complete, well written, and reflects that in the fact that each function is a separate stand-alone program. Shell, which serves as a menu "front-end" to DOS and your network operating system, ties all the Office pieces into a whole functional unit. If your application software is WordPerfect "shell aware" and has the proper "hooks," as all WordPerfect Corporation programs do, you can "hot-key" switch from program to program, using Shell's built-in clipboard if you want to move data between files. Otherwise, you can use Shell to menu into any program, but you have to exit that software to get back to the Shell menu and run other programs. The Shell also has

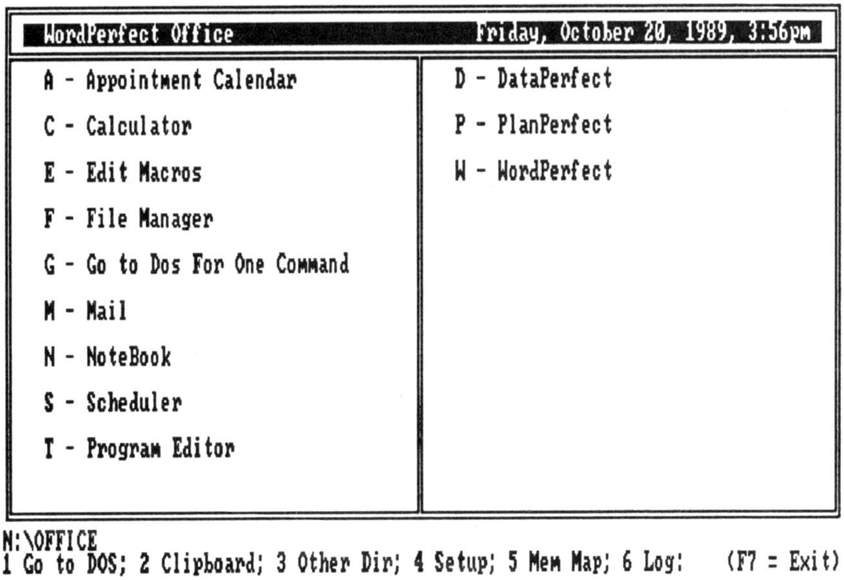

```
┌─────────────────────────────────────────────────────────────────────┐
│ ▐WordPerfect Office▌                    Friday, October 20, 1989, 3:56pm│
├───────────────────────────────────┬─────────────────────────────────┤
│  A - Appointment Calendar         │  D - DataPerfect                │
│                                   │                                 │
│  C - Calculator                   │  P - PlanPerfect                │
│                                   │                                 │
│  E - Edit Macros                  │  W - WordPerfect                │
│                                   │                                 │
│  F - File Manager                 │                                 │
│                                   │                                 │
│  G - Go to Dos For One Command    │                                 │
│                                   │                                 │
│  M - Mail                         │                                 │
│                                   │                                 │
│  N - NoteBook                     │                                 │
│                                   │                                 │
│  S - Scheduler                    │                                 │
│                                   │                                 │
│  T - Program Editor               │                                 │
│                                   │                                 │
└───────────────────────────────────┴─────────────────────────────────┘
N:\OFFICE
1 Go to DOS; 2 Clipboard; 3 Other Dir; 4 Setup; 5 Mem Map; 6 Log;   (F7 = Exit)
```

Fig. 10-3. The Main menu for WordPerfect Office.

extensive macro capabilities, which are available to shell-aware programs.

As with all WordPerfect Corporation software, users who have any
experience with any one of its products will find learning WordPerfect
Office much easier than those with no such experience. All WordPerfect
Office modules adhere to the WordPerfect interface, which differs from
the rest of the PC world. For example, the F3 key calls up help, instead of
the industry standard, the F1 key, and the F7 key exits each module. All
the WordPerfect Office products have on-line help and all show important
command key actions on the bottom line, as shown in Fig.10-4,which
contrasts with WordPerfect itself and its infamous almost blank screen.

The WordPerfect Office modularity, which provides one of its great
strengths by letting you adjust the programs you need, also provides one
of the software's biggest weaknesses of just too many bits and pieces. For
example, the personal calendar and the scheduler are separate programs.
Both packages do read the other's files and display events noted in their
opposite number. But, for example, the scheduler only tells you that
something has been scheduled in the calendar, not the details of the event.

The WordPerfect Office mail system works well, with the editor
appearing to be a small subset of WordPerfect itself. The Mail screen is
shown in Fig. 10-5. You can bold or underline text for affect, but you
can't do any block operations. Because the mail editor does import files,

```
MAMCAL.FIL              Friday, October 20, 1989              3:58pm
```

```
Sun Mon Tue Wed Thu Fri Sat           Friday, October 20, 1989
┌──┬──┬──┬──┬──┬──┬──┐              ═══════════ Memo ═══════════
│17│18│19│20│21│22│23│
├──┼──┼──┼──┼──┼──┼──┤
│24│25│26│27│28│29│30│
├──┴──┴──┴──┴──┴──┴──┤             ──────── Appointments ────────
│     October 1989   │
├──┬──┬──┬──┬──┬──┬──┤
│ 1│ 2│ 3│ 4│ 5│ 6│ 7│
├──┼──┼──┼──┼──┼──┼──┤
│ 8│•9│10│11│12│13│14│
├──┼──┼──┼──┼──┼──┼──┤
│15│16│17│18│19│■ │21│             ──────── To-Do List ────────
├──┼──┼──┼──┼──┼──┼──┤
│22│23│24│25│26│27│28│
├──┼──┼──┼──┼──┼──┼──┤
│29│30│31│  │  │  │  │
├──┴──┴──┴──┴──┴──┴──┤
│    November 1989   │
├──┬──┬──┬──┬──┬──┬──┤
│  │  │  │ 1│ 2│ 3│ 4│
└──┴──┴──┴──┴──┴──┴──┘
```

```
CALENDAR  Version 2.0  (C)Copyright 1985,1988  WordPerfect Corporation
```

Fig. 10-4. WordPerfect Office appointment book.

```
WP Mail:MARK                  Friday, October 20, 1989  3:59 pm
```

```
┌─ IN BOX ──────────────────────────────────────────────────────┐
│ PAUL           04/05 10:54  This is new mail                   │
│                                                                │
│                                                                │
│                                                                │
│                                                                │
│                                                                │
│                                                                │
└────────────────────────────────────────────────────────────────┘
┌─ OUT BOX ─────────────────────────────────────────────────────┐
│        Empty Mailbox                                           │
│                                                                │
│                                                                │
│                                                                │
│                                                                │
└────────────────────────────────────────────────────────────────┘
```

```
Tab OUT box;
1 Read; 2 Info; 3 Save; 4 Delete; 5 Mail; 6 Group; 7 Phone Msg; 8 Options: 1
```

Fig. 10-5. The Mail screen for WordPerfect Office.

you can use WordPerfect for creating text and then import it for transmission. The WordPerfect Office mail system also has a phone message function.

Of the remaining WordPerfect Office programs, the calculator is excellent, offering more power than some separately purchased calculators we've seen. The Macro Editor, allows you to easily edit macros for all WordPerfect Corporation software, including WordPerfect, but not DataPerfect, which has no macro capabilities of its own (it must use Shell macros). The Programming Editor (PE), while making life easier for WordPerfect users who also want to edit software source code, falls short of the worthwhile mark by not having word-wrap. Because it's so much smaller and quicker loading than WordPerfect, the PE should offer an excellent resource for those small ASCII files we all have to work on now and then. But without word-wrap, if you're not a programmer, you'll probably only find PE useful for writing occasional batch files.

Installing WordPerfect Office

You must manually install WordPerfect Office by copying files from the five distribution disks into a directory, which you create, and by performing several chores for configuration and installation of users. The process, which requires you to proceed step-by-step through detailed instructions, is exacting. Surely the manufacturer could automate setup to make installation much easier. Though installation may be detailed, this is promised to be easier in future versions of the product.

AUTHORS' RATINGS

We feel **The Coordinator II** and **WordPerfect Office** are the best two of these five groupware programs. The Coordinator II offers a unique approach to work group integration, while WordPerfect Office offers the best combination of features and implementation. We rate **Higgins** and **Office Works** second because they offer excellent alternatives to The Coordinator II and WordPerfect Office, if you don't need the former's unique capabilities, or want to learn the WordPerfect user interface. **Right Hand Man** may prove viable for a small network of advanced users who are willing to put up with its quirks, but at this stage of its development, we really must rate it at the bottom.

Electronic Mail

ELECTRONIC Mail has become an increasingly important aspect of networking. The ability to compose messages and send them to other users on the network has become one of the more important media for office and corporate communications. With more and more offices approaching, or achieving a 1 to 1 ratio of staff to PCs, Electronic Mail (E-Mail) will become an even more important networking task.

Selecting an E-Mail system is extremely important. The user interface is virtually as important as the list of features that a particular E-Mail package has to offer. There are a number of E-Mail packages available now in the market. This chapter is designed to take an in-depth look at what we believe is the state-of-the-art in E-Mail. We've found DaVinci Mail to be both an advanced E-Mail package with many excellent features, and one which is especially well designed and implemented.

DAVINCI MAIL
INSTALLATION AND ADMINISTRATION

DaVinci Mail installation is as easy as placing the installation diskette in Drive A: and typing Install. The program is definitely NetWare-aware. DaVinci Mail creates its own subdirectories, copies files to the appropriate places on the server disk, and sets the proper file flags and directory rights.

After DaVinci Mail completes its installation, you, as the LAN manager, have to run the ADMIN program. ADMIN sets the overall configuration of the mail program, adds and deletes users, and sets passwords, colors, etc.

You also use ADMIN to maintain mailing lists, which are simply named groups of people who are part of a mailing list. For example, you might have a mailing list called "technicians," made up of Bill, George and Sam. Simply addressing an E-Mail message to "technicians" automatically creates messages to each person in the group.

As a LAN-aware package, DaVinci Mail uses the existing NetWare user and group lists as a starting point to construct its lists. The program includes each NetWare user as a DaVinci user. If users are NetWare group members, they become DaVinci group members automatically.

Using DaVinci

You'll find DaVinci Mail about as intuitive as you can get in a software package. If you set up the system properly, simply typing EMail from anywhere on the LAN brings up the program. DaVinci knows who you are from your login name and takes you directly to your messages. If you desire to pop into the program from another person's workstation, type EMail *username*, where *username* is your DaVinci name.

Upon entering DaVinci, a user first sees a list of the waiting messages. Use cursor keys to move the light bar to the message you want to read, press the Enter key, and DaVinci displays the message on the screen shown in Fig. 11-1. You have several choices at this point, as shown in Fig. 11-2. You can go forward or backward in the message list, as well as answering the mail directly from this screen.

An excellent feature of the responding to a message option, is the split screen that keeps the message you're responding to on the top half of the screen, as shown in Fig. 11-3. Although you cannot see the entire message, you can see the address and subject information. Other choices include forwarding the message to another recipient or saving to a file. To forward a message simply hit the forward key and select the new recipient. Saving the message to a file provides a convenient way of saving the text of a long message in a file for inclusion in a letter, report, or other document.

To create a message, simply highlight the F2-CREATE! option from the top menu. From this point on it's just fill-in-the-blanks. You can use mailing lists (groups of users who are members of a group), or select individual recipients from a bounce bar menu (see Fig.11-4). Even the most novice computer user will be able to build messages easily and quickly using the intuitive DaVinci user interface.

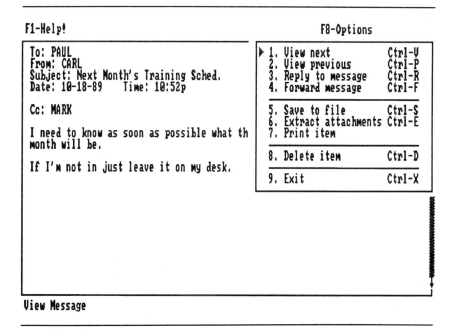

F1-Help!   F2-Create!   F3-Mailbox   F4-System   F5-Names   F6-Setup

```
Status From          ▶ 1. View message    Ctrl-V     Date    Time
                       2. Reply to message  Ctrl-R
1---    CARL           3. Forward message   Ctrl-F     10-18-89 10:52p
1---    MARK                                            10-18-89 10:50p
1---    JAN            4. Save to file                  10-18-89 10:48p
                       5. Extract attachments Ctrl-E
                       6. Print item        Ctrl-P
                       7. Print list
                       8. Search mail       Ctrl-S

                       9. Delete item       Ctrl-D
```

Mailbox: PAUL

Fig. 11-1. Choosing the message you want to read.

F1-Help!   F8-Options

```
To: PAUL                         ▶ 1. View next        Ctrl-V
From: CARL                         2. View previous    Ctrl-P
Subject: Next Month's Training Sched. 3. Reply to message  Ctrl-R
Date: 10-18-89    Time: 10:52p     4. Forward message   Ctrl-F

Cc: MARK                           5. Save to file      Ctrl-S
                                   6. Extract attachments Ctrl-E
I need to know as soon as possible what th  7. Print item
month will be.

If I'm not in just leave it on my desk.   8. Delete item       Ctrl-D

                                   9. Exit              Ctrl-X
```

View Message

Fig. 11-2. The View Message screen with options for further action.

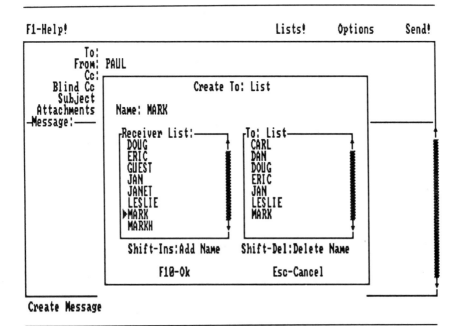

```
F1-Help!                        F7-Lists!   F8-Options   F9-Send!
┌Original:─────────────────────────────────────────────────────────┐
│To: PAUL                                                            ▲
│From: MARK                                                          █
│Subject: The Morgan and Morgan Project                             █
│Date: 10-18-89    Time: 10:50p                                     █
│                                                                   █
│Cc: STEVE                                                          ▼
├───────────────────────────────────────────────────────────────────┤
│        To: MARK                                                   │
│      From: PAUL                                                   │
│        Cc:                                                        │
│  Blind Cc:                                                        │
│   Subject: Re: The Morgan and Morgan Pr                           │
│Attachments:                                                       │
├Message:───────────────────────────────────────────────────────────┤
│Let me offer my assistance and support on this project.  Whatever you need, ▲
│just let me know.  This would be a nice one to close this month!   █
│                                                                   █
│Best regards,                                                      █
│                                                                   █
│                                                                   █
│                                                                   █
└───────────────────────────────────────────────────────────────────┘
Reply to Message
```

Fig. 11-3. The Reply to Message screen splits so you can view the letter while writing a response.

```
F1-Help!                         Lists!    Options    Send!
┌──────────────────────────────────────────────────────────────┐
│       To:                                                     │
│     From: PAUL                                                │
│       Cc:                                                     │
│ Blind Cc     ┌──────────Create To: List──────────┐           │
│  Subject     │                                    │           │
│Attachments   │ Name: MARK                         │           ▲
├Message:──    │                                    │           █
│              │┌Receiver List:──┐ ┌To: List───┐    │           █
│              ││ DOUG           █ │ CARL       █    │           █
│              ││ ERIC           █ │ DAN        █    │           █
│              ││ GUEST          █ │ DOUG       █    │           █
│              ││ JAN            █ │ ERIC       █    │           █
│              ││ JANET          █ │ JAN        █    │           █
│              ││ LESLIE         █ │ LESLIE     █    │           █
│              ││▶MARK           █ │ MARK       █    │           █
│              ││ MARKH          █ │            █    │           █
│              │└────────────────┘ └───────────┘    │           █
│              │ Shift-Ins:Add Name  Shift-Del:Delete Name       █
│              │                                    │           █
│              │    F10-Ok            Esc-Cancel    │           █
│              └────────────────────────────────────┘           │
└──────────────────────────────────────────────────────────────┘
Create Message
```

Fig. 11-4. The Create Message menu offers the options to create a mailing list or send to individual recipients.

Because one of DaVinci's more powerful features includes attachments with message, the program can also convert attachments back to files. To send a copy of this chapter in non-ASCII word processor format to one of the co-authors for editing or review, the writer simply attaches the file to a message saying, "Hey, look at this!" After editing, the file is returned with a reply message. Extraction pulls the file out from its DaVinci message file and deposits it on the disk in the form of a file in the directory of your choice. Attachments are created using the "Build Attachments List" option. DaVinci will list the files and directories on your disk which you just highlight and select (see Fig. 11-5).

As a NetWare-aware program, DaVinci Mail uses the Novell notification system to advise users that a message has arrived. Because this RAM-resident feature can negatively affect some programs, you might want to turn this feature off for workstations running TSR-sensitive applications.

Advanced Features

DaVinci Mail has some very nice advanced built-in features. One, *Draft Mode*, gives you the capability to save a partially finished message, for editing later. You can use this feature in several ways. One way saves partially completed memos, prior to actually sending them. Another way

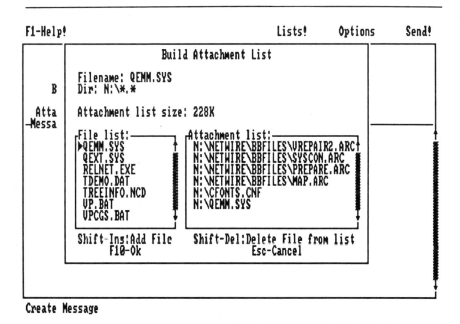

Fig. 11-5. The Build Attachments List option.

sends a message today, then another tomorrow as a reminder or to a totally different person.

DaVinci includes a *Handling* feature, that gives first, second and third class mail options. You'll primarily use this for sorting messages. Other options include *Priority*, which delivers a message immediately. Priority also certifies messages, which automatically returns them to the sender noting the date and time that the message was read by the recipient.

DaVinci also has an advanced encryption option. When normal NetWare security is inadequate, users can send encrypted messages. Set the encrypt flag in the handling menu and DaVinci Mail will prompt the user for an encrypt password that must be entered by the recipient to read the message. The encrypt password acts as both a public key and an access password.

Another interesting feature of DaVinci Mail, Bulk Mail, sends mail to a large mailing list (like EVERYONE). This feature dispatches copy to the "Bulk Mail Server," which takes on the task of sending the mail to each recipient. This is not a standard feature and requires that a bulk mail server be set up.

DaVinci Mail also includes the E-Mail *Clipboard*, which is a special memory buffer that enables the easy copying of text from one area to another while editing messages.

More Powerful Features

Internet, the DaVinci Mail wide area routing program, allows multiple servers to be linked on a backbone of networks. Internet can also link multiple networks in different locations over standard phone lines.

DaVinci is also compatible with the Message Handling System (MHS) that comes bundled with Novell NetWare. With MHS, you can integrate many office tasks. For example Ashton-Tate's Framework III is MHS-compatible, as is SYZYGY from Information Research, and The Coordinator from Action Technologies. Using this message handling system, various locations and programs can all communicate with each other using one standardized method.

In addition, DaVinci Mail will have links to other environments, that the manufacturer is developing in the form of gateways. Links to MCI Mail, Fax machines, PROFS, etc., should ensure that most installation won't outgrow this product.

SUMMARY

There are many good E-Mail packages on the market which can provide this important function to a Novell LAN. Overall, we have found that DaVinci Mail offers a very powerful EMail package with an intuitive, easy-to-use design. The program's underlying power and capability, should prove more than adequate to keep the most demanding user happy. From the opening screen, to the first message to use on a daily basis, users will be impressed with the DaVinci product's excellent, thoughtful interface.

PART V

Menuing Systems and Front-ends

Menuing

NETWARE comes with a menu utility that many users use because it comes with NetWare and it is easy to use and set up. It works by creating text files with the menu options and a set of instructions on what to do if that option is chosen.

To begin working with the Novell menu let's first take a look at the Example menu supplied with NetWare. To run this example you need a search path set up to the public directory and must have read, open, search, delete and create rights to the current directory.

With this done, type MENU MAIN at the DOS prompt. NetWare will bring up the menu shown in Fig. 12-1. This menu presents choices to all of Novell's non-command line utilities. If you press the up and down arrows you will be able to move the bounce bar to the chosen item and press return to select the item. You will also notice that the menu looks and feels just like all the other Novell utilities. This is the major benefit of using this menu system besides the fact that it is included with the operating system. After going in and out of the selected utilities, press the Esc key to get to the exit prompt and select Yes to exit. Figure 12-2 shows the menu command file, MAIN.MNU, that was just executed.

NOTE: You can press the Alt-F10 key combination to exit at any point in the menu system. This also works for all the Novell utilities.

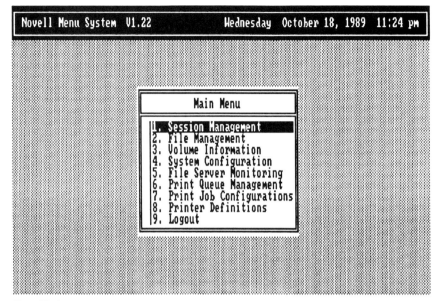

```
Novell Menu System  V1.22          Wednesday  October 18, 1989  11:24 pm
```

```
                        ┌────────────────────────────┐
                        │         Main Menu          │
                        ├────────────────────────────┤
                        │ 1. Session Management      │
                        │ 2. File Management         │
                        │ 3. Volume Information      │
                        │ 4. System Configuration    │
                        │ 5. File Server Monitoring  │
                        │ 6. Print Queue Management  │
                        │ 7. Print Job Configurations│
                        │ 8. Printer Definitions     │
                        │ 9. Logout                  │
                        └────────────────────────────┘
```

Fig. 12-1. Novell's Menu utility.

```
%Main Menu,0,0,3
1. Session Management
      Session
2. File Management
      Filer
3. Volume Information
      VolInfo
4. System Configuration
      SysCon
5. File Server Monitoring
      FConsole
6. Print Queue Management
      PConsole
7. Print Job Configurations
      PrintCon
8. Printer Definitions
      PrintDef
9. Logout
      !Logout
```

                                        Doc 1 Pg 1 Ln 1.37" Pos 1"

Fig. 12-2. Novell's Menu command program.

This command file is a pure ASCII text file located in the public directory. To alter it or to create one for yourself, you must use a text editor capable of producing a pure DOS text file. Editors that produce this by default are EDLIN, WordPerfect's Program Editor (PE), Solutions Systems Brief, and many shareware editors including SemWare's QEdit. Many word processors also provide an option of producing a DOS test file. The menu system will not work with word processor files. Make sure your word processor can produce this kind of output.

Novell's example menu shows us the general format of all menu files. The first line of the command file names the menu and gives three parameters. The first two show the upper left coordinates where the menu will be located. The third is the Palette number it will use for the color. If no coordinates or the coordinates 0,0 are specified then MENU will center the options in the middle of the screen.

The next commands are the menu options and their associated commands. The menu options start in the first column and can begin with any alpha-numeric character. It is sometimes necessary to number these options because they will be listed in alphabetic order when displayed on the screen. By numbering the options you are ensured that they will be displayed in the order you enter them.

The second line is indented and contains any command that can be put into a DOS batch file. When the MENU program processes this information, it takes all the lines that are indented and places them into a batch file for execution. After execution the batch file terminates and the MENU program returns the user to the same place in the menu where they exited.

When you choose an option from the Novell MENU, it will create two files in your default directory. These files are GO###.BAT and RESTART.###. The ### will be replaced by your connection number. For example, if you are logged in to connection 1 the two files will be GO001.BAT and RESTART.001. If you abnormally exit an application called by the menu then you might see these files build up on your system. If you see these files out on your network that begin to age, you might want to delete them as you see them. They do not take up much room but can clutter directory space and make directory management more complex.

Additional Menu Commands

There are some commands that are not supported by DOS batch files but that the MENU system will interpret before releasing execution to the batch file. These commands allow for logging out of the system and for variable placement in the MENU command.

Logging Out with Menu

Because access to the network is denied when a user logs out, a batch file cannot be used to exit from the network. Therefore, you must use a command built into the network system, which is !LOGOUT. When the MENU program encounters this command it does not create the batch files but unloads itself from memory and logs the uses out of the system.

Variables within the Menu Commands

Some programs need commands given to them at the time of execution from the command line. These are programs like NCOPY and NDIR. MENU that let you prompt for this information with the @ symbol within the MENU command file. The syntax of the @ command is:

```
command @#"input prompt for data"
```

The # sign is replaced by a number representing the variable name. You can have up to nine variables. MENU will display a prompt box displaying the question in quotes asking the user for the data. For example:

```
%Sample input menu
NDIR
   ndir @1"Enter drive/filename" @2"Enter NDIR options"
   pause
```

You can reuse the same variable more than once within your command option. Using variables can add more capability to your menu system.

Novell Menu Usage

The Novell MENU system is easy to understand, and provides a standard interface to present to users. It does not include security, error tolerance, or any advanced features that a menu system should have. Because of this, there have been several third party programs published that are substantially more powerful than Novell's MENU. One of the most powerful is the Saber Menu system.

SABER MENU SYSTEM

The Saber Menu System, an advanced menuing system from Saber Software, provides a user interface especially tailored for extremely efficient operation in the Novell environment.

A major concern to network managers and users, is how do you conserve RAM resources? As programs grow larger and larger, the room available for network shells and Terminate Stay Resident programs (TSRs), such as Borland's SideKick, has become greatly squeezed. One of Saber's chief benefits is that it can produce a user-interface menu system without any overhead. Saber requires as little as 0K RAM to operate. Well actually, that's not totally true, because all software requires RAM to operate. However, when you select an application program from a Saber menu, the menu-interface program saves its operating environment to a disk and unloads itself, freeing all RAM for the application.

Saber's design uses standard bounce-bar menus controlled by the cursor keys (see Fig. 12-3). Saber offers support for nested menus up to 10 deep. The program can maintain up to 99 different menus. You create each menu using either Saber's built-in editor or a standard ASCII editor. Before you can use a Saber menu, the program must compile it. The Saber compiler is very fast and converts the menu source file to a file with a .DAT extension.

You define Saber menus using a relatively simple menu control language, which contains a set of command verbs and a set of allowable parameters. You can enter your menu scripts either through a DOS text editor or through the Saber Menu Update program (see Fig. 12-4). The command line takes the following format:

COMMAND *Action* {*parameters*}

The commands include the following:

Command	*Description*
MENU	*Defines the start of a new menu*
ITEM	*Labels a menu item*
SHOW	*Displays a sub-menu*
EXEC	*Passes command to DOS for execution*
GETO	*Prompts for and gets an optional parameter*
GETR	*Prompts for and gets a required parameter*
LOAD	*Like show except from an external menu file*
PSWD	*Password access to a menu item*

For example, the small program:

ITEM WORDPERFECT
EXEC WP

shows WordPerfect on a menu and executes the command WP anytime you select the menu item.

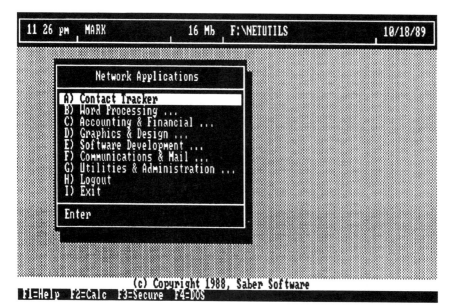

Fig. 12-3. Sample Saber Menu screen.

Fig. 12-4. Saber Menu Update screen.

You include parameters shown within brackets at the end of the command line. These parameters include items such as:

Parameter	Description
PAUSE	Asks user to strike a key to continue
NOECHO	Represses the "Loading ProgramName" message
BATCH	Removes menu system from memory before executing
NOCLEAR	Prevents screen clear before executing item
CHDIR	Forces menu system to change drive and dir
SHOW	Displays DOS command name

and give additional control to the menu system.

As a full-featured menu and management system, Saber comes with some additional features that make it especially useful to network managers. For example, Saber includes several programs that you can use in and outside of a menu system. These include SECURE, a program that locks up a workstation until a password is reentered as shown in Fig. 12-5. A user, who might want to leave a work active while going for lunch, executes SECURE from a Saber menu or from the program's TSR mode to protect an active workstation from all but re-booting.

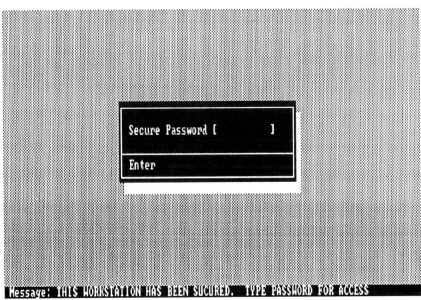

Fig. 12-5. The menu display when the Saber SECURE program is running.

For network managers, the program METER can be a real boon. METER tracks how many users are accessing a particular software package at any time, to be able to ensure compliance with licensing restrictions of version of networkable software. Figure 12-6 is an example of the information provided by METER. METER uses data files that use a dBASE-type file structure to control these functions. The following set of menu commands limits the number of Lotus 1-2-3 users to five:

```
ITEM Lotus 123 { }
EXEC METER LOGIN LOTUS123 \ USAGE \ AUDIT.DBF 5
EXEC IF ERRORLEVEL = = 1 GOTO exit
EXEC CD X: \ LOTUS
EXEC LOTUS
EXEC METER LOGOUT LOTUS123 \ USAGE \ AUDIT.DBF – A
EXEC :exit
```

The program SIZE gives a complete directory listing with a date, time, size (in both used and allocated), and attributes. Other programs include COLDBOOT and WARMBOOT, that can re-boot a computer system from a batch file or menu. Another Saber program, YESNO, prompts for a "Yes or No" response and sets an operating system error level to be used for future batch file processing.

Saber also comes with a very handy calculator. Saber borrowed a

```
Meter v1.01, (c) Copyright 1988 Saber Software

Usage: Meter LOGIN    Application MeterFile MaxUsers {Project} -p -a
       Meter LOGOUT   Application MeterFile -a
       Meter RECORD   Message     MeterFile {Project} -p
       Meter CLOSE    Application MeterFile {"message"}
       Meter OPEN     Application MeterFile -a
       Meter RESET    MeterFile -a
       Meter LIST     MeterFile {status} -i
       Meter STATUS   MeterFile

Notes: -p, Prompt for project ID
       -a, Keep audit information
       -i, Display using international date format

Application: 1-20 character application name (must be one word)
MeterFile  : Path and file specification for meter control file
MaxUsers   : Number of Users allowed in application at one time
Project    : 1-20 character project name (must be one word), optional

F:\NETUTILS>
```

Fig. 12-6. Information provided by the Saber METER program.

concept from the Apple Macintosh computer world in designing its menu system. In addition to choices of fare, Saber menus have a set of user-definable "Desk Accessories," which are accessed from function keys while the menu is on the screen. For example, a user might set up the F2 key to implement the Saber calculator.

The Saber Menu System has many capabilities. The documentation isn't particularly well organized and menus are harder to set up than they need be, primarily because of the language/compiler approach, which isn't very intuitive. If you choose the Saber Menu System, be prepared to spend some serious time reading and experimenting to get your menus working properly. These minor shortcomings notwithstanding, we recommend the Saber Menu System as an appropriate third-party menu system for all sizes of NetWare installations. Saber's own menu screens are well laid out and easy to understand and its overall design is quite good. Compared to the built-in NetWare MENU system. Saber has a lot to offer.

OTHER NETWORK MENU SYSTEMS

Many companies have started releasing menu systems for the Novell environment. On Novell's NetWire Forum on CompuServe there are several demo and shareware packages that you can download and try out. With the complexity of a network, menus are going to play a larger part in the distribution of network services. In the future we should be able to have centrally defined items and have them distributed to all servers on the network. Today we can give the users a simple menu that allows for security, ease of use, and accounting features that allow for simple and efficient network operation.

PART VI

Supplemental Software

Network Utilities

ONE of the most prolific areas of software development for LANs has been in the arena of utility software. There are many sources of network utility software. One excellent source is the Novell SIG on CompuServe called NetWire. There are many excellent Public Domain and Shareware programs that we have found to be of great value and interest. There are also an ever-growing number of commercial developers producing very innovative and useful utilities. The pages of LAN Magazine, LAN Times, LAN Technology and others, are filled with commercial utility products.

While the entire gamut of network utilities is beyond the scope of this book, we nevertheless thought it beneficial to highlight one commercial vendor's family of utility products. Fresh Technology is a developer devoted to producing LAN utility products. Their product line includes MAP Assist, LAN Assist and Printer Assist.

PRINTER ASSIST

Printer Assist enables a local workstation printer to function as a network printer. You'll find several reasons for using a locally attached printer as a network printer. Because Novell only supports five shared printers (two serial, three parallel), any LAN needing more has a real problem. Furthermore, parallel printer cables have a severe length restriction—approximately 15 ft. Even serial printers cables are limited to about 150 ft. Because local area networks can span up to 16,000 ft or more, printer cable limitations can pose real problems.

Users often find it rather inconvenient to walk long distances to the file server to retrieve printed material. Consider a large corporate network spread out over several floors in a building, or between several buildings in a campus layout. The time wasted when users leave their general work areas to retrieve printouts lessens much of the productivity increase offered by computers and LANs.

Some large businesses might require several laser printers, numerous dot-matrix printers, and maybe even a few high speed printers to all operate off the same server. When this happens, LAN managers usually install a *print server.* Print server software monitors a file server print queue and shuttles print jobs off to a workstation printer for local printing. With this type of software, printers no longer have to be physically attached to the network file server.

You'll find two types of print servers. As with the two kinds of file servers, print servers can be *dedicated* or *non-dedicated.* Where a LAN requires a high volume of print services or where many different printers are needed, a dedicated server makes sense. On the other hand, if the network users only do limited printing at local printers, non-dedicated print servers are better. Printer Assist allows either or both types of print server on a LAN. When you run Printer Assist on a workstation, it simply monitors a file server queue for any print files that it has been directed to service.

How Printer Assist Works

Printer Assist, actually a small TSR program, monitors designated queues on the file server. When a job enters the queue, Printer Assist routes the job to the local printer, so the job is printed as though it were physically attached to the file server. Printer Assist is an extremely efficient program, taking up only 4672 bytes of RAM when monitoring a single queue for a single local printer.

You may control multiple printers from a single workstation simply by loading multiple copies of the program. To load Printer Assist simply type PA at the DOS prompt, any command line parameters. As with other Fresh Technology products, typing the program name followed by a "?" list the available command line options and syntax. The following is the result:

PRINTER ASSIST

Resident Print Server
Copyright 1987 Clay L Jones
Ver - 3.0A Serial Number - PXXXXXXX

```
PA  –          REMOVE PA FROM MEMORY
PA  ?          DISPLAY HELP FOR PA
PA  C = #      MULTIPLE COPIES OF PA AT ONCE
PA  S = #      SERIAL PORT NUMBER (COM1 - COM4)
PA  S = X#     SERIAL PORT HEX ADDRESS DIRECTLY
PA  B = #      PARALLEL PRINTER VIA BIOS CALLS
PA  O = #      SERIAL PORT SETTINGS (SEE TABLE BELOW)
PA  P = #      PARALLEL PORT NUMBER (LPT1 - LPT3)
PA  P = X#     PARALLEL PORT HEX ADDRESS DIRECTLY
PA  M = #      MAX CHARACTERS PER SECOND
PA  F          FULL SCREEN DISPLAY OF PA STATUS WITH
               UPDATING
PA  V          DISPLAY THE CURRENT PA STATUS
PA  T = #      NUMBER OF SECONDS BETWEEN POLING QUEUE
PA  L = FILE   FILE NAME TO WRITE A LOG OF PRINT JOBS TO
```

QUEUE SELECTION FOR NETWARE 2.1
PA Q(1-3) = [SERVER/]QUEUENAME
  SERVER/ IS AN OPTIONAL SERVER NAME.
  QUEUENAME IS THE NAME OF THE QUEUE TO MONITOR.
  QUEUE NAMES CAN BE FOUND BY PCONSOLE. IF MULTIPLE
  QUEUES ARE SPECIFIED ANY JOBS IN Q1 WILL BE PRINTED
  BEFORE JOBS IN Q2 ETC.

Here's a couple of examples that should make it extremely clear how easy Printer Assist is to set up. This command line loads Printer Assist to monitor the Print Queue PRINTQ_2 on Server FS1. It routes the print job to serial port 1:

```
PA Q1 = FS1/PRINTQ_2 S = 1
```

The following command loads Printer Assist to monitor Print Queues HPLJET1 on Server FS1 and HPLJET3 on Server FS2. It routes the print job to the parallel port located at hex address 378. The queue is polled once every 15 seconds:

```
PA Q1 = FS1/HPLJET1 Q2 = FS2/HPLJET3 P = X378 T = 15
```

After setting up your print server with Printer Assist, the next step defines authorized "users." Use the program PAQADD which needs the syntax, PAQADD QUEUE_NAME USERNAME. Thus,

```
PAQADD HPLJET3 PAUL
```

makes Paul an authorized user of the HPLJET2 queue at the local work-station. To revoke this authority, merely use the Novell PCONSOLE program.

Dedicated Printer Assist

You invoke the dedicated print server version of Printer Assist by typing the program named PAD. This acronym for Printer Assist Dedicated brings up a print server screen shown in Fig. 13-1. The console screen for the print server allows for both the monitoring and the management of the print server. PAD can easily handle functions such as backing up the printer a line, a page, or more, and printing a character or a line. The program also makes switching printers very easy.

Needed information for the print server is maintained in a file called PAD.DAT, which is merely an ASCII file that details the printers and the parameters for the server. The syntax is essentially the same as for the non-dedicated mode.

A utility program called PACONFIG writes both the command line for a non-dedicated print server and the PAD.DAT file for a dedicated print server (see Figs. 13-2 and 13-3). Using the familiar Novell menu utility model, this program allows the user to simply select options such as printer type, printer configuration, destination server and queue, printer description and log file, all using a point and shoot interface.

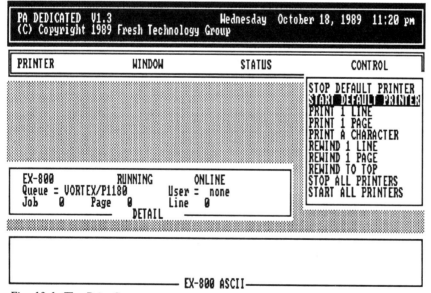

Fig. 13-1. The Print Server screen.

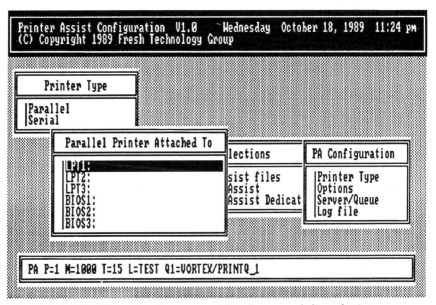

Fig. 13-2. PACONFIG writes the command line for a non-dedicated print server.

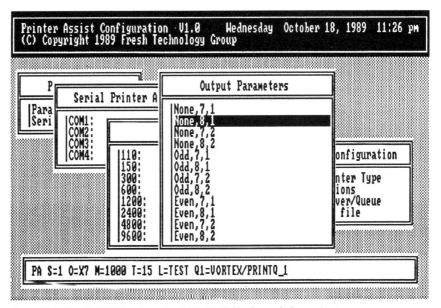

Fig. 13-3. PACONFIG writes the PAD.DAT file for a dedicated print server.

One step that you might easily miss, is using the PAQADD program. This makes a user the print server. Look at it like this: before my printer can be the network printer, I (Tom) must be designated as a print queue server. The command line looks like this:

PAQADD LASER_Q TOM

This makes the NetWare user Tom's workstation the print server for the network print queue LASER_Q.

Printer Assist allows the use of a log file, which records statistics for each print job serviced by the shared local printer. The file records the User, Server, Date, Time, Size, Form Feeds and Line Feeds serviced. You'll find this an important management tool for managing print resources on a network. Implement the log file by including the switch /L = FileName.Ext with the PA command line. The report from this log file is generated with the program PAREPORT.

With Printer Assist running, simply type PA to get the Printer Assist status screen. This screen is shown in Fig. 13-4.

Printer Assist is one of our favorite network printer utilities. It is small, efficient, feature laden, and very cost effective.

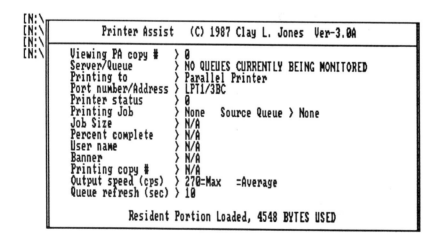

Fig. 13-4. The Printer Assist status screen.

MAP ASSIST

Map Assist is one of those why-didn't-somebody-think-of-this-before utilities, that potentially has a myriad of uses. Map Assist simply allows a local workstation hard disk drive to be used as a network drive. That is, you can have access to not only the standard suite of network drives available on a NetWare server, but also other local workstation drives as well. Before getting into the specifics of how the product works, let's look at a couple of uses.

The first important use for this product allows you to back up local drives across the LAN. Normally, NetWare only allows you to back up network file servers to a tape drive attached to a workstation. You can't back up other local workstation drives to that designated network backup workstation. Because Map Assist allows a local drive to be seen as a network drive, you can back up individual workstations' hard disk drives to the same designated backup tape drive.

One company we know of actually set up a dedicated machine to be used as a "Backup Server." Using Lan Assist, a computer user sets in motion the backup process for all servers and workstations in a single operation—all with a single tape backup device and without leaving his desk.

Additionally, Map Assist conveniently allows CD-ROM drives (large unerasable optical drives), and WORM drives (large write only optical drives) to be used on a LAN. The Novell 255-megabyte volume limitation causes one of the major problems for using this type of drive. If you want to use one of these drives on a server, normally you must partition it into multiple 255-megabyte volumes. While this works with most WORM and erasable laser drives, CD-ROM drives do not offer this capability. To use a CD-ROM on a NetWare LAN using Map Assist, simply set up a workstation (dedicated or non-dedicated) with the drive attached and configured as a local drive. Map Assist then allows access as though it's a network drive.

Setting Up Map Assist

Map Assist has two components. The first is the "host" portion; the second, the "workstation" portion. The host portion sets up communications with the network, which allows the host to share its disk drive (or portions thereof) with others on the network. The command line format is:

```
MAR d: \ [directory] RW = USER RO = SRVR/USER RW = GROUP
```

The various components of the command line respectively are: d: \ directory is the drive and directory that is to be mapped to a network drive; RO specifies that this is to be read only; RW is read/write. Note that you can give access by group, as well as by individual.

Map Assist allows a great deal of flexibility and security to the LAN Manager. First, a user must log onto the network and be in an eligible group or a named person to have access to the mapped drive. For security, a user can have read only access, to prevent unauthorized or inadvertent corruption of the data on the mapped drive.

The second portion of Map Assist, the workstation portion, has the command line format:

MA d: = [SERVER/]USER

For example, typing in the command line MA X:JOHN creates a logged drive X: on the local workstation, that points to the drive user JOHN made available with the MA command above.

Rather than using command line options, you'll find it easier to use the workstation portion of Map Assist with its menu option. Type MA /M to start the Map Assist workstation in menu mode (See Fig. 13-5). Tell Map Assist the drive you want to MAP and the program gives you a list of users (See Fig. 13-6). If that user has Map Assist loaded and you are authorized to use the drive, that local drive/volume becomes a mapped network drive just like any other.

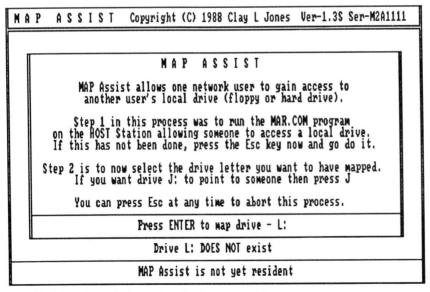

Fig. 13-5. The Map Assist workstation in menu mode.

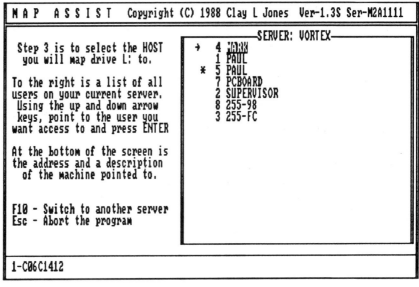

Fig. 13-6. List of users on drive that has been selected for mapping.

You'll find Map Assist an elegant little utility that has uses as widely varied as the imaginations and needs of NetWare users.

LAN ASSIST

LAN Assist has become indispensable to many LAN administrators. LAN Assist allows a person at one workstation to view and control another workstation computer on the LAN. Screens and keystrokes pass transparently back and forth along the network from the assisted station to the assisting station.

You'll find LAN Assist has two primary uses. As the name implies, LAN Assist was originally designed to allow a LAN manager or a network support person to provide assistance and technical support to LAN users without going to their physical location. When a user is experiencing difficulty, you only have to fire up LAN Assist and you can see exactly what is happening on the user's workstation to provide real-time help.

Another important use for LAN Assist provides what we like to call "hardware multi-tasking." You can utilize unused workstations or dedicated machines on the network as "task servers" where you can pass jobs. For example, you want to handle a time consuming job, such as creating multiple indices for a 50-megabyte database. You keep your own machine available for personal use, by passing that job off to another machine. LAN Assist allows that type of remote workstation control without leaving your desk.

Another example, we use LAN Assist in our office to control a bulletin board system (BBS). We don't even have a monitor or keyboard installed in the unattended BBS station. We just use LAN Assist to provide occasional routine maintenance on the BBS machine as needed. We also use LAN Assist in conjunction with a remote dial-in program, such as PC Anywhere. We generally maintain a dedicated dial-in workstation for remote access to our LAN. Then, using LAN Assist, we can get from that machine to any workstation on the LAN and run it as though we are sitting at the desk in front of it.

LAN Assist has two components. The first, the *host* component, allows a manager to assist at a user's workstation. The user types in "LA +", which loads a TSR that takes just slightly over 2K RAM. This allows the manager's remote station to provide assistance.

The second component provides *support*. Simply typing LA brings up a menu (see Fig. 13-7) that allows the manager to select the user's workstation.

The LAN Assist display appears just a little jerky, particularly when viewing a screen that's doing a great deal of scrolling, such as using the DIR command on a large subdirectory. You get this because screen information passes along the network in packets. The higher the network load the more pronounced the effect caused by the packets.

You'll find installing LAN Assist Plus very straightforward. Because the needs of individual installations can vary widely, the program has a

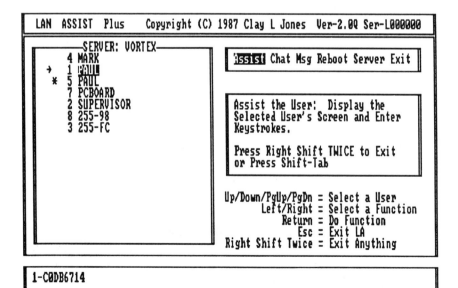

Fig. 13-7. Selecting the user's workstation.

long list of options for configuring it to meet your needs. The utility LACONFIG controls the following:

- Allow keys to be entered remotely.

- Pass scan codes directly to user end.

- Allow remote re-boot.

- Display watching user name.

- Allow watched user to terminate look.

- Allow resident portion to be removed.

- Recognize LAN Assist group members.

- Users not logged in can use LA.

- By default allow anyone to assist any computer.

- Allow the LAN Assist group to use the /D option.

- Allow LAN Assist to run while being LAN Assisted.

- Allow multiple users to assist one computer.

- Select key to pop up the Chat Screen.

- Select key to pop up the LAN Assist Menu.

You can change many of these options at run time.

SUMMARY

The arena of NetWare utilities is growing at a phenomenal rate. If you have identified a need in your own network management arena, chances are that someone has already written a utility to handle the need. The Fresh Technology utilities provide an introduction to the type and quality of network utilities in the marketplace.

PART VII
Other NetWares

14

NetWare for VMS

DIGITAL Equipment Corporation's (DEC) Virtual Address eXtended (VAX) line of computers pretty much dominates the minicomputer market. With quality products and services, DEC has led the minicomputer industry, with many of their machines installed in both small and large companies. These same companies have been participating in the PC networking boon of the past few years with NetWare LANs. With the introduction of NetWare for VMS, Novell bridges the gap to the DEC community forming a heterogeneous network of resources, transparently available to NetWare users.

Novell's current release of NetWare for VMS is version 2.01, which is a port of the 2.0a PC NetWare operating system to VMS versions 4.6, 4.7, and 5.x. The VAX port offers normal NetWare PC-type file and print server functions, along with a Terminal Emulation Service (TES). The file and print services work just as on a PC server, where the user executes the NetWare shell and switches to the network drive. Then, they LOGIN and usually never know that the host is a VAX and not a PC server running NetWare for VMS.

NETWARE FOR VMS SERVICES

The DEC Virtual Memory System (VMS) uses processes to allocate network resources. These processes are programs that run on the VAX to handle different tasks. NetWare for VMS runs as one of these processes.

As a process, it must abide by whatever restrictions the VAX system manager has placed on it. The VAX uses a User Authorization File (UAF) to control security. During the NetWare for VMS installation, you give the Novell software a user profile for the UAF. The UAF controls user access by the restrictions in that profile.

Most users must abide by this profile, but NetWare for VAX does allow Hybrid users who have their own VMS user profile, if it is higher than NetWare's. When this happens, NetWare does not control security. Security is left to the Normal VMS operating system. This process could actually allow a hybrid user to have more rights than the NetWare supervisor. Although, the NetWare LAN manager (supervisor) is usually the same as the VAX system manager.

FILE AND PRINT SERVICES

Files on the VAX look the same to the DOS user as they do to the VMS user. NetWare handles any necessary translation. Users can access any file on the VAX that can be seen by DOS. If a file doesn't conform with DOS naming conventions, you must rename it to access it—more on this later.

You handle print services by connecting a NetWare printer number to a VMS print queue or batch queue. One nice feature about VMS, is that it supports up to 255 printers, a great improvement over the PC-NetWare limit of 5. NetWare for VMS also comes with a print symbiont, which is used for large print jobs, large graphic files or just more efficient printing with NetWare for VMS.

TERMINAL EMULATION SERVICES (TES)

NetWare for VMS has a Terminate Stay Resident (TSR) program that redirects interrupt 14, the serial port BIOS call, through the Ethernet to the VAX server. If you run TES on your Workstation-PC, the program watches for any communication for the VAX. The VAX NetWare driver treats your PC just like a directly connected terminal. While TES itself is not a terminal emulation package, it allows a PC-based DEC terminal emulation package to function with the LAN. Thus, the LAN lets PCs work as VAX terminals without other directly connected terminal cables or intermediary terminal services. TES allows better PC/VAX communication management with only a single cable to each workstation that provides both network and VAX terminal services. Appendix C lists TES-compatible terminal emulation packages.

NETWARE FOR VMS USERS

NetWare for VMS allows three types of users: 1) NetWare only users, 2) VMS only users, and 3) hybrid users needing both services. *NetWare only* users access the VAX just as if it was a PC-based NetWare server. These users can take advantage of VAX printers and disk storage. They also do not need a VMS account and will probably never use TES.

VMS only users are just the opposite. They may have a guest account under NetWare if TES is loaded. However, aside from loading TES, they spend all their time logged onto their VMS account.

Hybrid users combine NetWare and VAX use. They may have files in both environments and may frequently switch back and forth between DOS and VMS. These users can actually have both services available at the same time if they use a memory resident terminal emulator. NetWare for VMS defines these hybrid users only as a user name. When they enter the NetWare system, they receive a password of < VMS_USER >, which tells NetWare the person is a VMS user. NetWare does not store a password for this user, but passes the user name and password through to the VAX UAF for authorization. At this point, all the user's UAF restrictions are enforced.

SYSTEM REQUIREMENTS

A VAX system must meet several requirements before NetWare for VMS can be installed:

- It must be a processor that Novell currently supports —almost all VAX processors are supported.

- It must run VMS operating system versions 4.6, 4.7, or 5.x.

- It must have a minimum of two megabytes of RAM, although four megabytes is strongly recommended.

- It must have at least 7000 blocks (3.5 megabytes) of permanent disk storage available, with an additional 7000 blocks free for temporary working space during installation.

- NetWare requires a TK50 or 9 track, 1600 BPI tape unit from which to load the installation programs.

- If LAN users are to be able to print, VAX print queues must be set up and working properly.

- A DEC or DEC-compatible Ethernet controller must be installed and attached to an Ethernet network.

- A batch queue must be in operation on the VAX to start the NetWare for VMS process.

- The VAX/VMS rights database must not contain the ITNS$ACCESS identifier. Because NetWare for VMS reserves this identifier, it must be available for the LAN software to operate. If it exists, this identifier should be deleted before NetWare for VMS installation.

INSTALLATION PROCEDURE

NetWare is installed for VMS on the VAX using the VMSINSTAL utility located in the SYS$UPDATE directory. The Novell VAX LAN software comes on a single tape and installation is not complicated. During installation, NetWare for VMS asks for a few specifications about the system, then takes care of everything except inserting commands in the VAX startup file for automatic operation. We strongly recommend that you have the VAX system completely backed up before starting the NetWare for VMS installation. Although NetWare is not likely to cause damage to your system, it's a poor system manager who plays with fate.

If you have any questions before installing NetWare for VMS, be sure to double check the manuals or with the dealer who sold the product. Beause of the intricacies of the product and the complexities of the platform where it is being installed, you should be confident of all aspects of installation beforehand.

NOTE: To emphasize these installation precautions, we must inform you that Novell has a special certification class for dealers who sell this product.

To begin, login under the SYSTEM account with the tape in the tape drive and on-line. Then, execute the VMSINSTAL utility by typing:

```
@SYS$UPDATE:VMSINSTAL
```

The software asks you the following questions during installation:

1. **The location of the VMS distributions tape?** Normally this is MUA0 but, depending on your system configuration, it can vary.

2. **The products that will be processed?** This can either be the name NETWARE_VMS or an * indicating all products on the tape. NetWare is the only product supplied on the tape.

3. **Are you ready?** Confirmation of installation. Type Yes to continue.

4. VMSINSTAL then displays some information about the installation process. Read this information and press the Enter key to continue.

5. **Do you wish to purge the files replaced by this installation [YES]?** Unless this is an update and you wish to keep the old files answer Yes or just press the Enter key.

6. **Name of the NetWare file server [VAX]?** Name your file server per your own environment. For most, VAX is a good name.

7. **Specify the NetWare Common directory?** This defaults to SYS$COMMON:[NETWARE_VMS] and should not be changed unless this is special installation.

8. **Specify the NetWare Specific directory?** This defaults to SYS$SPECIFIC:[NETWARE_VMS_FILES] and also should not be changed unless this is a special installation.

9. **Specify product startup File directory?** This defaults to the SYS$MANAGER: directory.

10. **Specify system volume directory:** This defaults to SYS$SYS-DEVICE:[NETWARE_VMS_SYS_VOLUME] and if needed can be changed.

11. **Ethernet Controller type?** Depending on your VAX model, this can vary. NetWare makes a best guess at the default. The following are valid Ethernet Controller types as defined in the NetWare for VMS manual:

Ethernet Controller	*Computer type*
DEBNT	BI bus VAX
DEBNA	BI bus VAX
DEUNA	Unibus VAX
DELUA	Unibus VAX
DEQNA	Qbus VAX
DELQA	Qbus VAX
DESVA	MicroVAX 2000

12. **Ethernet device type?** This depends on your Ethernet controller. The following are some valid device types as defined by the NetWare for VMS manual:

Ethernet Controller   Device Type Names

DEBNT	ETA, ETB, etc.
DEBNA	ETA, ETB, etc.
DEUNA	XEA, XEB, etc.
DELUA	XEA, XEB, etc.
DEQNA	XQA, XQB, etc.
DELQA	XQZ, XQB, etc.
DESVA	ESA, ESB, etc.

13. **NetWork number?** Enter the 8-digit hexadecimal number that corresponds with the NetWare Ethernet segment you will connect. This number must match the network number of your NetWare PC server, if there is another one attached to the network.

14. **File Server Guest Account?** As discussed earlier, NetWare users not defined under VMS fall under any limitations that are placed upon the NetWare account. Here it asks for a name to associate with this account.

15. **File Server Guest Account password?** Enter any password. It will only be used during the startup of the NetWare process to gain access to it files.

16. **Enter a unique UIC for the [GUEST] account?** This is the User Identification Code for NetWare only users. This should not be the SYSTEM account. An example of a volute ID is [100,100].

17. **Console Program Password?** If you wish to secure the console from being operated by other system operators, you can place a password on it. If no password is desired press the Enter key.

18. **Batch Queue for starting the server?** The default of SYS-$BATCH should be used unless there is another, more suitable, batch queue.

After entering all this data, NetWare for VMS gives you a chance to look over your parameters and change any that have been mistyped or that need to be changed. After answering No to more changes, NetWare for VMS begins the installation using those parameters.

STARTING NETWARE FOR VMS

The command file for starting NetWare for VMS is located in the directory specified during installation. If it has been changed, replace the specified directory with your actual directory. The command to start NetWare for VMS is @SYS$MANAGER:STARTNWVMS.COM, which loads and initiates the IPX/SPX drivers and starts the VAX server process. You can put this command in the SYSSTARTUP in the SYS$MANAGER directory for automatic startup, when the VAX is booted.

When NetWare for VMS loads, you see three device drivers load, QX, QT, and QB. Then a message similar to:

Job NW_DETACH_SRV (queue SYS$BATCH, entry 10) started on SYS$BATCH

is displayed, which shows that the process has been given to the batch queue to be processed. When done, the system displays the following message notifying you that the batch job has been completed:

Job NW_DETACH_SRV (queue SYS$BATCH, entry 10) completed

Once it's initiated, you should see the NetWare for VMS process with a SHOW SYSTEM command. Once running, all standard NetWare for VMS services are available to LAN users.

ERRORS

If your server does not start at this point there are several things to check:

1. Did you change the SYSGEN parameters as recommended in the book? Novell recommends the following parameters be changed:

   CHANNELCNT = 1000
   GBLPAGES and GBLPAGFIL increased by 1500
   VIRTUALPAGECNT = 20000
   WSMAX > 2000

2. Check the LOG files that are contained in the NWVMS$SPECIFIC directory, which record any errors encountered while the NetWare for VMS process initiates. Reviewing these files might give a clue to the reason for the error.

NETWORK CONFIGURATION

Now that you have NetWare for VMS running, you should think about your network configuration. First, outline your network configuration and decide how your users are going to log onto the network. Most LANs that incorporate NetWare for VMS servers are quite large and already have a backbone with several subnets. If this is your case, your users will most likely log on through either an internal or external NetWare bridge, or an Ethernet bridge of some type. We recommend that you break your users into subnetworks for access.

ETHERNET OR 802.3?

Before you are able to see the VAX as a server, you must alter either the bridge, server, or shell LAN driver that connects to the VAX, because of a slight difference between Novell's use of the IEEE 802.3 implementation and the DEC, Intel, and Xerox (DIX) implementation from which the 802.3 spec received its origin. These three companies adopted the Ethernet standard when the IEEE committee decided to create the 802.3 standard. The IEEE took the Ethernet standard and made it fit the International Standards Organization/Open System Interconnect (ISO/OSI) model. By doing so, they altered the spec slightly.

The major difference between these two standards is the packet frame format. The Ethernet standard specifies a protocol-type field as opposed to 802.3 which specifies a length field. DEC is migrating towards 802.3 compliance starting with DECnet Phase V, but will also continue to support the Ethernet standard. Because Novell is committed to supporting all communications standards, the company will also support both standards.

ECONFIG

Novell utility to configure LAN drivers to both of these standards is called ECONFIG. ECONFIG can take a driver and format it to use either the length field or Novell's unique protocol type number 8137. Xerox, who administers the Ethernet protocol types, assigned this as the number assigned to Novell.

Depending on your configuration, you can have either a bridge that has one 802.3 LAN driver and one Ethernet (type 8137) driver or just configure all your workstations to be Ethernet type. We recommend the first choice, because it involves less work and stays more with Novell's default use of the IEEE standard.

To configure the LAN driver, you must first have a compatible Ethernet driver that can be ECONFIGed. Most manufacturers have altered their LAN drivers and have added the letters EC to the end of the LAN driver's name. If you try to ECONFIG a driver that does not conform to this specification, ECONFIG returns an error message.

Using ECONFIG

When ECONFIG runs without any parameters, it gives you general usage. You receive the following message:

```
C:\SHGEN>econfig
 Usage: econfig [volume:] file [parameter list]
 [parameter list] is one of the following:
 SHELL:[configuration type]
     A-D:[configuration type]
         [configuration type] = N, E [type constant]
         [type constant] = :0-FFFF (8137 is Novell's assigned
                                   :type constant)
 Example:   :econfig os.exe a:n; b:e 8137; c:e 15af
            :econfig shell.com shell:e 8137
```

To ECONFIG your shell program, use the following syntax:

```
ECONFIG ipx.com shell:e 8137
```

This assigns Novell's type to the shell and lets it talk to the VAX server, which can also be done through a bridge in a file server or external bridge. Below is an example of a server running ARCnet as LAN A and Ethernet as LAN B which is to be connected to the backbone. The second example has an external bridge that connects an Ethernet segment to the backbone. Both are similar, except for the name of the program to be altered:

- ECONFIG net$os.exe a:n; b:e 8137

- ECONFIG bridge.exe a:n; b:e 8137

USING NETWARE FOR VMS

NetWare for VMS has a few differences that are worth noting. First, NetWare for VMS is only a 2.0a implementation of NetWare, which presents a few inconveniences that people had to deal with before NetWare 2.1 was released. With 2.1, Novell changed the way printing functions are handled and added more functionality. They introduced new printing commands, CAPTURE and ENDCAPTURE, that replaced the 2.0a SPOOL and ENDSPOOL. This would not be a great problem, except the new 2.1 commands cannot be used on 2.0a servers. In reverse, the 2.0a commands do not work on 2.1 servers. So, you have to know what server you'll print with and execute the appropriate print command. When the 2.1 revision of NetWare for VMS is introduced, this problem will be alleviated.

FILE NAMING CONVENTIONS

Because of the difference between VMS and DOS file names, NetWare for VMS has to interpret naming conventions on both sides. VMS allows many parameters when specifying a directory name. The VMS format is:

device:[directory.subdirectory.subsubdirectory] filename.type;version

where the parameters are:

device   The logical or physical name of the disk or tape containing the file (i.e., SYS$MANAGER, SYS$DISK, etc.)

directory   Up to 39 alphanumeric characters for the names of directories. VMS names may not contain a % or *. Directories and subdirectories are enclosed by brackets.

subdirectory   Up to 7 subdirectories can be separated by periods. They fall under the same naming restrictions as directories.

filename   VMS filenames can be up to 39 characters long, with the same naming restrictions as directories.

type   Type of file, which is similar to DOS file extensions. Same restrictions as directories. Some samples are EXE, CMD, and COM. Directories have the type DIR and otherwise appear as normal VMS files.

version   VMS does not automatically delete a file when it is written over or replaced. It keeps the old versions numbered sequentially until purged from the system.

NetWare uses an expanded DOS naming convention. NetWare's format is:

volume: \ *directory* \ *subdirectory* \ *filename.ext*

Where the parameters are:

Volume	A NetWare volume can be up to 14 characters long. NetWare names volumes with alphanumeric characters.
directory	Alphanumeric up to 14 characters. Most directory names conform to the DOS naming convention of 8 characters followed by a period followed by a 3-character extension. NetWare allows any 14 characters except \ / ? , ; : .
subdirectory	Same as directory.
filename	NetWare allows file names to have 14 characters. Most files that are created under DOS conform to an 8-character file name.
Extension	DOS uses extensions to describe the type of file names. NetWare sees the extension as just part of the file name.

Wildcards

Both DOS and VMS allow for wildcards:

DOS	*VMS*	*Functions*
?	%	Matches a single character
*	*	Matches one or more characters

CONSOLE COMMANDS

The NetWare for VMS console provides many of the same features as the Advanced NetWare PC console. You'll find three significant additional commands. Also, some commands cannot be supported either fully or partially because of the way NetWare is implemented as a client operating system. Some NetWare commands that pertain to printing devices have been replaced by Digital Command Language (DCL) commands. We will describe the new commands and give a reference to the DCL commands. But for a detailed listing of each command and its use, consult your NetWare for VMS manager's guide.

To bring up the NetWare for VMS console, type the following at the command prompt:

```
RUN NWVMS$COMMON:NW_CNSL
```

After running console, you're prompted for the server name, which is the name of your NetWare for VMS server. After entering the server name, you see a colon, which is Novell's monitor prompt. You can execute the following commands at that prompt.

HELP   Help, a feature that should have been added to the PC server operating system, is an on-line help utility that lists and explains each console command.

CONNECT NWVOLUME   Connect a NetWare volume to a VMS directory to connect a user's VMS directory for access from NetWare. You can connect any directory on the VAX as a NetWare volume for access by DOS users. When you connect a volume, you can either specify it to conform to MS-DOS or NetWare's naming conventions. The syntax and an example with abbreviation are given below:

CONNECT   NWVOLUME = *volume_name:*/VMSDIRECTORY = *directory_name* /STANDARD = *standard*

    CONN NWVOL = MARK: /VMSDIR = DUA0:MARK /S = N

You can also have NetWare volumes connected automatically during startup of the NetWare for VMS process by creating and putting the same syntax into an OPTIONS.DAT file located in the NWVMS$SPECIFIC directory. If you have changed either the location or the name of this file in the NW_SRV.CMD file, refer to it for the option file's name and location.

CONNECT PRINTER   Connects NetWare printers to VAX print queues or batch queues. You can connect a printer interactively from the console or, as with CONNECT NWVOLUME, you can connect it during the startup of NetWare for VMS. The syntax and example are listed here:

    CONNECT PRINTER # /QUEUE = *queue_name*

    conn print 1 /queue = sys$print

SUMMARY

NetWare for VMS represents Novell's first attempt at a portable NetWare operating system. We see it as the harbinger for Portable NetWare. NetWare for VMS is a good operating system that achieves a functionality unequaled in the PC LAN environment. Installation is easy and on-line help is always available from the installation utilities. Once installed, NetWare for VMS is very flexible. It allows many changes to be made to its operating environment with no major work. The Terminal Emulation utilities allow easy access to VMS programs from any station on the network with little strain on VMS resources.

Appendices

Appendix A
NetWare Resources

USER GROUPS

Novell user groups have been sprouting up all over the United States and in many other countries. This is the best place to find ongoing support from other individuals charged with the same task. Look in a local computer paper or other publication that lists user groups in your area or contact Novell at 800-453-1267 and ask for User Relations.

NetWire

NetWire is a Novell Special interest group on CompuServe. Here you will find some of the best talent and experience with the NetWare operating system. The System operators are experienced NetWare administrators and installers that lend their time to answer users' questions. Novell technical support and product managers also monitor and answer questions. The only charge is for the regular on-line time of CompuServe.

CompuServe
Customer Service
P.O. Box 20212
Columbus, OH 43220
(800) 848-8990

PUBLICATIONS

LAN TIMES (McGraw-Hill's Network Users Publication)
151 East 1700 South
Suite 100
Provo, Utah 84606
(801) 379-5800

LAN TIMES is one of the oldest and best of the NetWare-specific magazines. It was started by Novell and, in the middle of 1989, sold to McGraw-Hill. It is published monthly and free to qualified subscribers.

NetWare Advisor (The Independent Journal of NetWare Management)
24 Greenway Plaza
Suite 1305
Houston, TX 77046-2401
(713) 965-9000

NetWare Advisor is a newsletter that is packed full of tips, tricks, techniques, and tutorials every month. Each article is something you can apply as you read it. It costs $69 per year.

NetWare Technical Journal
122 East 1700 South
P.O. Box 5900
Provo, Utah 84606
(801) 379-5900

This is the detailed technical specifically tailored for the needs and concerns of technical system managers, programmers and others with an interest in the inner workings of NetWare. Mainly focused at developers, this monthly magazine can help you understand the how and why of Novell's NetWare. It costs $50 per year.

LAN (The Local Area Network Magazine)
12 West 21 Street
New York, NY 10010
(212) 206-6660

Networking, reviews, and tutorials make this a good overall publication. Articles cover the general networking industry. $19.97 per year.

LAN TECHNOLOGY
501 Galveston Drive
Redwood City, CA 94063
(415) 366-3600

Straightforward articles with good examples every month. It costs $29.97 per year.

Appendix B
NetWare Command Summary

The Novell NetWare Command Line utilities are located in the Public Directory. They are used for a wide variety of reasons from Logging in to the Network, copying files, and changing file attributes, to Logging back out. In this appendix is a reference list of the command line utilities with their syntax and usage. Novell devotes an entire manual to these utilities, so you are referred to that volume for detailed technical questions about the utilities.

ATTACH
ATTACH [SERVER[/USER]]

This command will provide a connection to another server attached to the same network. It will not disturb the existing connection and it will not execute a login script on the ATTACHed server. This is normally followed with a MAP command to make a volume on the ATTACHed server available.

CAPTURE
CAPTURE [option list]

Capture is used to redirect printing to a network printer. The CAPTURE option list is easily displayed by typing CAPTURE ?. The options are shown below (Note: The shorthand abbreviations are obtained by typing only the Capitalized letters in the option. For example, the No Tabs option would be NT and the CReate shorthand would be CR):

Option	Description
SHow	Displays the current capture configuration
Job = *jobname*	Specifies the name of the job (used by Printcon).
Server = *servername*	Specifies the server that is to service the captured printing.

Queue = *queuename*	Specifies the Queue that is to service the print job.
Printer = *n*	Specifies which network printer is to service the print job.
Local = *n*	Used to indicate which local printer is to be captured. For example, L = 3 would indicate that the local LPT3 is to be captured.
Form = *n*	Indicates which form is to be used to print the job. Form definitions are created in Printcon.
Form = *formname*	Same as above but with a form name rather than a number.
CReate = *filename*	Redirects printing to the specified file rather than to a printer.
Copies = *n*	Will automatically print the number of copies specified. By handling the number of copies here, rather than in the application, can reduce the sizes of the queue files substantially.
TImeout = *n*	The time that the queue is to remain idle before closing the active queue and sending the file to the printer. Normally a value of about 10-15 seconds is a good starting point.
Keep	If this option is selected, the queue file is not automatically deleted when the printing is completed.
Tabs = *n*	The number of spaces that the Tab character is to be expanded.
No Tabs	Tells the queue to pass tab characters through unchanged. Always use No Tabs (NT) when printing graphic applications.
Banner = *text*	Up to 12 characters that appear on the banner. Default is LST:
NB	This option suppresses the printing of a banner.

NAMe = *text*	Specifies the username that is to appear in the upper half of the banner page. The default is the users login name (Login _Name).
FormFeed	Enables the issuing of a formfeed at the end of the print job. In many cases this is a waste of paper and can be turned off with NFF.
No Form Feed	Suppresses the printing of a formfeed at the end of a print job.
Autoendcap	Using this option, the print job is directed to the network printer upon exiting or entering an application. Default setting is Autoendcap ON.
No Autoendcap	Suppresses the Autoendcap feature.

A sample Capture command line is shown here with abbreviated options:

    CAPTURE J = 1/S = FS1/Q = PRINTQ_1/C = 2/TI = 10/NB/NFF/L = 2

This command line redirects the printing from the local printer port LPT2: to queue PRINTQ_1 on file server FS1. The Job number is 1, the timeout value is set to 10, formfeeds are suppressed, as are banners. To end capturing and return printing to local mode, use the ENDCAP command.

CASTOFF
CASTOFF [ALL]

This command is used to suppress the display of messages from other users on the workstation display. If you do not want to be disturbed, or more importantly, if the messages interfere with the application(s) you are running, then just type CASTOFF at the DOS prompt. This will not stop console broadcast.

CASTON
CASTON

This command re-enables the messaging system.

CHKVOL
CHKVOL [path]

CHKVOL is the NetWare equivalent of the DOS command CHKDSK. It will show the amount of total volume space, the amount used by files, the amount remaining, the bytes available to the particular user and the number of directory entries available on disk. Wildcards can be used. For example, CHKVOL * gives the above information for all current server volumes and CHKVOL */* executes CHKVOL for all network volumes for all attached servers. Figure B-1 shows an example of the CHKVOL command.

```
F:\PUBLIC>chkvol

Statistics for fixed volume VORTEX/SYS:
    267386880 bytes total volume space,
    252534784 bytes in 10015 files,
     14852096 bytes remaining on volume,
     14852096 bytes available to user MARK,
         6753 directory entries available.

F:\PUBLIC>chkvol vol1

Statistics for fixed volume VORTEX/VOL1:
     54296576 bytes total volume space,
     18931712 bytes in 822 files,
     35364864 bytes remaining on volume,
     35364864 bytes available to user MARK,
         3018 directory entries available.

F:\PUBLIC>
F:\PUBLIC>
F:\PUBLIC>
F:\PUBLIC>
F:\PUBLIC>
F:\PUBLIC>
```

Fig. B-1. A CHKVOL command example.

ENDCAP
ENDCAP [option]

ENDCAP is used to terminate capturing to a network printer. Like CAPTURE there are a number of options available. These are:

Option	*Description*
Local = *n*	Ends the Capturing of the specified local LPT port
ALL	Ends Capturing for ALL ports
Cancel	Ends the capturing of LPT1 and discards current print data
CancelLocal = *n*	Cancels Capturing of the local printer LPT port. Specifies and discards current print data
Cancel **ALL**	Cancels Capturing of all LPT ports and discards all printing data

FLAG
FLAG [path ¦ filespec[option]]

This command is used to change the flags on a file. When used by itself with no arguments, the command lists the current flags on the file. The possible file flags are shown below:

Flag	*Description*
S	Sharable
NS	Non-Sharable
RO	Read-Only
RW	Read Write
N	Normal (Non-Sharable and Read Write)
T	Transactional
I	Indexed

There are eight possible file attributes. In addition to the above attributes a file can also have attributes of System and Hidden. These attributes are not controllable by the FLAG command.

The only option for the command is the SUB option which will not only affect the files in the specified directory but also those in the subdirectories below. An example of the flag command is:

```
FLAG SYS:PUBLIC *.* NSRWIT
```

This changes the file flags for all of the files in the SYS volume, PUBLIC directory to NonSharable, ReadWrite, Indexed, Transactional.

FLAGDIR
FLAGDIR [path[option...]]

This is a new command effective with NetWare version 2.15. It allows the changing of attributes of subdirectories in a given directory. You must have Parental *and* Modify rights in the current directory to use the command. Like FLAG, FLAGDIR when entered without arguments, will list the current flags in the directory. Figure B-2 is an example of the FLAGDIR command. The available options for the command are as follows:

Option	Description
N	Normal
H	Hidden
S	System
P	Private

```
VORTEX/SYS:PUBLIC
   !NETWARE.NFO     Shareable    ReadOnly
   TUTOR.BAT        Shareable    ReadOnly
   LCONSOLE.EXE     Shareable    ReadOnly
   START.DBD        Shareable    ReadOnly
   _FILE_C.DBD      Shareable    ReadOnly
   _FILE_H.DBD      Shareable    ReadOnly
   RDEMO.EXE        Shareable    ReadOnly
   _FILE_F.DBD      Shareable    ReadOnly
   _FILE_B.DBD      Shareable    ReadOnly
   _FILE_A.DBD      Shareable    ReadOnly
   _FILE_G.DBD      Shareable    ReadOnly
   _FILE_D.DBD      Shareable    ReadOnly
   _FILE_E.DBD      Shareable    ReadOnly
   CASTON.EXE       Shareable    ReadOnly
   REVOKE.EXE       Shareable    ReadOnly
   FILER.EXE        Shareable    ReadOnly
   SYSCON.EXE       Shareable    ReadOnly
   NDIR.EXE         Shareable    ReadOnly
   FCONSOLE.EXE     Shareable    ReadOnly
   MAKEUSER.EXE     Shareable    ReadOnly
   MAKEUSER.HLP     Shareable    ReadOnly
   CAPTURE.EXE      Shareable    ReadOnly
```

Fig. B-2. Sample output of the FLAGDIR command.

GRANT
GRANT option [FOR path] TO [USER] user ¦ [GROUP] group

Normally users are added and Trustee rights are maintained using the Syscon utility. However, there are times when a command line method is much more efficient. GRANT allows the system manager to change rights "on-the-fly". The available rights are as follows:

- Read
- Write
- Open
- Create
- Delete
- Parental
- Search and Modify
- Modify

For example,

GRANT ROS FOR Q: TO JAN

gives Read, Open and Search Rights in directory Q: to user JAN.

HOLDOFF
HOLDOFF

HOLDOFF is used to reverse the effect of HOLDON.

HOLDON
HOLDON

Used to hold open files that you want to access.

LISTDIR
LISTDIR [path] [option]

Used to view subdirectories from any directory. Also lists the maximum rights mask. Options include:

Option	*Description*
/S	To view entire tree structure
/R	To show the maximum rights mask
/D	To view the creation date
/A	To view all

LOGIN

LOGIN [server/[user[option...]]]

Login is the command that is used to establish a connection to the file server and identify the user, verify passwords and begin execution of the login scripts. When used by itself, it will prompt for the username and password. To login to a specific server enter a command line like:

LOGIN FS1/PAUL

If there are multiple servers on your network and your login script attaches you to these, LOGIN will attempt to synchronize passwords among the servers.

NOTE: If you use LOGIN to attach to a server when you are already attached to another server, you will be logged out of the current server. You can ATTACH to multiple servers, but you can only LOGIN to one.

LOGOUT

LOGOUT

Logout terminates the session with the server and places the user in the LOGIN directory.

MAP

MAP
MAP [drive]
MAP path
MAP drive: = [drive \ path]
MAP Insert drive: = [drive \ path]
MAP DEL drive:
MAP REM drive:

The forms of the MAP command on the previous page are all available. MAP by itself displays the current drive Mapping. MAP X: will show the volume and directory that is pointed at by drive mapping. To define a new drive mapping use a command like MAP F: = SYS: \ UTIL. To remove a drive from the current mapping use MAP DEL or MAP REM. Figure B-3 is an example of the MAP command.

NCOPY
NCOPY filespec[TO] [path] [filename] [/Verify]

NCOPY is essentially a network replacement for the DOS COPY command. The command line syntax is essentially identical, as well. The DOS COPY command will function just fine in the network environment, however the NCOPY command will reduce the network traffic dramatically. If you copy a file from one logical drive to another on the same file server, the actual copy will take place on the server. The DOS COPY by contrast will move the file to the workstation conducting the copy and then back to file server.

NDIR
NDIR [path] \ [filename]
NDIR path \ filespec option[...]

NDIR is used to search and view the contents of various directories and subdirectories on the network. The options can be grouped into various

```
F:\PUBLIC)map

Drive   A: = VORTEX/SYS:LOGIN
Drive   F: = VORTEX/SYS:PUBLIC
Drive   G: = VORTEX/SYS:
Drive   K: = VORTEX/SYS:CONTACT
Drive   L: = VORTEX/VOL3:
Drive   M: = VORTEX/VOL1:
Drive   N: = VORTEX/VOL2:OFFICE
        -----
SEARCH1: = Z:. [VORTEX/SYS:PUBLIC]
SEARCH2: = Y:. [VORTEX/SYS:PUBLIC/IBM_PC/MSDOS/V3.30]
SEARCH3: = X:. [VORTEX/SYS:UTILITY]
SEARCH4: = W:. [VORTEX/SYS:WP50]
SEARCH5: = V:. [VORTEX/SYS:EMAIL/MAILUSER]
SEARCH6: = U:. [VORTEX/VOL2:LOTUS]
SEARCH7: = T:. [VORTEX/SYS:MARK]
SEARCH8: = S:. [VORTEX/SYS:ATC/EXE]
SEARCH9: = R:. [VORTEX/SYS:MHS/EXE]

F:\PUBLIC)
```

Fig. B-3. Sample output of the MAP command.

categories. The options are shown below. For additional information, see the Command Line Utilities Manual. Figure B-4 is an example of the NDIR command.

```
SYS:PUBLIC
File Name      Size    Last Modified    Accessed Created  Flags       Owner
------------   -------- ---------------- -------- -------- ---------   ----------
!NETWARE NFO   1126400  1-01-96   2:08a  10-11-89 1-04-89  [R----S-]   SUPERVISOR
!NETWARE WIN        232 1-01-96   2:08a  10-11-89 1-04-89  [R----S-]   SUPERVISOR
10355163 $$$        318 10-08-89 10:36a  10-11-89 10-08-89 [W------]   PAUL
10362854 $$$        318 10-08-89 10:36a  10-11-89 10-08-89 [W------]   PAUL
APPIMAGE PDF        292 1-05-89   5:05p  10-11-89 1-01-85  [R----S-]   SUPERVISOR
APPLASER PDF        201 1-05-89   5:05p  10-11-89 1-01-85  [R----S-]   SUPERVISOR
ATTACH   EXE      23847 1-05-89   5:00p  10-20-89 1-01-85  [W----S-]   SUPERVISOR
BOARD    BAT        439 9-08-89   3:09p  10-11-89 9-08-89  [W------]   PAUL
BREQUEST EXE      17361 2-22-88   1:35p  10-11-89 1-04-89  [R----S-]   SUPERVISOR
CAPTURE  EXE      35328 1-05-89   4:59p  10-20-89 1-01-85  [R----S-]   SUPERVISOR
CASTOFF  EXE      15383 1-05-89   5:04p  10-11-89 1-01-85  [R----S-]   SUPERVISOR
CASTON   EXE      11079 1-05-89   4:57p  10-11-89 1-01-85  [R----S-]   SUPERVISOR
CHKVOL   EXE      19255 1-05-89   5:00p  10-18-89 1-01-85  [R----S-]   SUPERVISOR
CIT120D  PDF        284 1-05-89   5:05p  10-11-89 1-01-85  [R----S-]   SUPERVISOR
CIT20    PDF        281 1-05-89   5:05p  10-11-89 1-01-85  [R----S-]   SUPERVISOR
CIT224   PDF        356 1-05-89   5:05p  10-11-89 1-01-85  [R----S-]   SUPERVISOR
CITOH310 PDF        286 1-05-89   5:05p  10-11-89 1-01-85  [R----S-]   SUPERVISOR
CITOH600 PDF        380 1-05-89   5:05p  10-11-89 1-01-85  [R----S-]   SUPERVISOR
CMPQ$RUN OVL       2248 1-05-89   4:59p  10-11-89 1-01-85  [R----S-]   SUPERVISOR
COLORPAL EXE      50176 1-05-89   5:01p  10-11-89 1-01-85  [R----S-]   SUPERVISOR

Press any key to continue ... ('C' for continuous)
```

Fig. B-4. Sample of the NDIR command.

Basic File Information

FILENAME [NOT] = file

OWNER [NOT] = name

ACCESS [NOT] BEFORE ¦ = ¦

UPDATE [NOT] BEFORE ¦ = ¦

CREATE [NOT] BEFORE ¦ = ¦

SIZE [NOT] GREATER THAN ¦ = ¦ LESS THAN nnn

File Attributes

[NOT] SYSTEM

[NOT] HIDDEN

[NOT] MODIFIED

[NOT] EXECUTE ONLY

[NOT] SHAREABLE

[NOT] READ ONLY

[NOT] INDEXED

[NOT] TRANSACTIONAL

Sort File Information

[REVERSE] SORT FILENAME

[REVERSE] SORT OWNER

[REVERSE] SORT ACCESS

[REVERSE] SORT UPDATED

[REVERSE] SORT CREATE

[REVERSE] SORT SIZE

View Only Information

Files Only

Directories Only

MAC

SUBdirectories

BRief

Archiving Information

BACKUP

WIDE

[NOT] ARCHIVED

ARCHIVED DATE BEFORE ¦ = ¦ AFTER

CHANGED

[NOT] ARCHIVED BIT

TOUCHED

Help

HELP

The command NDIR HELP will bring up a screen that summarizes all of the options listed above for NDIR.

NPRINT
NPRINT filespec [OPTION]

NPRINT is a command that sends the contents of a file directly to a network printer. The NPRINT options are the same as those for the CAPTURE command. NPRINT is often used in conjunction with capturing to a file. If you CAPTURE a long report to a file, you can then NPRINT it to the actual printer at a later time.

NSNIPES/NCSNIPES
NSNIPES/NCSNIPES

This is a network game which can be played alone or with multiple participants across the net. The NSNIPES is the monochrome version and NCSNIPES is the color version.

NVER
NVER

NVER displays information about the shell version, OS version, LAN Driver, File Server Name, and NOS version. This is shown in Fig. B-5.

PSTAT
PSTAT

PSTAT gives printer information for the current file server. This includes printer number, status, ready condition, and form number/name.

PURGE
PURGE

```
F:\PUBLIC)nver

The NetWare NetBIOS module is not loaded,
     unable to provide version information.

IPX Version: 2.15
SPX Version: 2.15

LAN Driver:  NetWare RX-Net  V1.00 (881010) V1.00
             IRQ = 2, I/O Base = 2E0h, RAM Buffer at D000:0

Shell:       V2.15 Rev. A
DOS:         MSDOS V3.30 on IBM_PC

FileServer:  VORTEX
    Novell   SFT NetWare 286 V2.15 Rev. A   12/11/88

F:\PUBLIC)
```

Fig. B-5. An example of the NVER command.

regain the disk space that they formerly occupied, use the PURGE command.

REMOVE
REMOVE[USER]user ¦ [GROUP]group [FROM] [path]

This command is used to remove a user or group from the trustee list of a given directory.

RENDIR
RENDIR path [TO] directory

RENDIR is a shortened form of Rename Directory and is used to actually rename a directory.

REVOKE
REVOKE

The REVOKE command is the opposite of the GRANT command. It is used to revoke trustee rights from a user or group in a given directory.

RIGHTS
RIGHTS [path]

RIGHTS will list all of a user's effective rights in a directory.

SALVAGE
SALVAGE

SALVAGE is a fantastic utility that has saved more than one system manager. SALVAGE can be used to restore an erased file or files on a network volume. A few simple rules must be followed.

- First, do not log out of the file server. Deleted files are automatically purged upon logging out.

- Do not create any new files or erase any additional files on the volume. Either of these actions also purges the files.

- Do not use the PURGE command.

- SALVAGE must be run at the workstation where the files were deleted.

SEND
SEND "message" [TO] [USER]
SEND "message" [TO] [GROUP]

This command will transmit the text string in quotes to the user or group across the network. The message will appear on the bottom line of the screen and will require a Ctrl-Enter to clear. This is not a replacement for E-Mail, but the SEND command is a quick, convenient way to get short messages across the network in real time.

SETPASS
SETPASS [server]

SETPASS allows users to set their passwords. Simply typing SETPASS will cause the program to prompt for the old password and then the new password.

SETTTS
SETTTS [logical level[physical level]]

SETTTS is used to initialize the Transaction Tacking System within SFT NetWare. Each level is a number from 1 through 255.

SLIST
SLIST

SLIST is a utility that is a shortened form of Server LIST. It is one of the few utilities that resides in the LOGIN directory. It enables the user to view the available servers that are currently on the net.

SMODE
SMODE [path \ filespec[option]]

The SMODE command will set the Search Mode. There are a number of optional search methods or modes that NetWare will follow. SMODE is used to change this mode. If you think your programs are not operating properly with respect to finding the files that they need to run, you should check the mode to see if changing the search mode will correct the problem.

SYSTIME
SYSTIME[server]

This command has two purposes. The first is to view the date/time on the current server. Simply type SYSTIME to view the system time. The second purpose is to synchronize your workstation with a particular server.

TLIST
TLIST[path[users ¦ groups]]

This command is used to view the trustee list for a given directory.

USERLIST
USERLIST[server/] [user] [/A]

USERLIST is used to see who else is logged into the network. When you use the /A option it will include the Network Number and Node Address of the user along with the Login Time, as shown in Fig. B-6.

WHOAMI
WHOAMI[server] [option]

You can use WHOAMI to view who you are on the network. It will tell you which server you are attached to, your user name on each, your login

```
F:\PUBLIC)userlist /a

User Information for Server VORTEX
Connection  User Name        Network    Node Address    Login Time
----------  ---------------  --------   ------------    ------------------
     1        JAN            [   250] [          2]  10-20-1989   4:38 pm
     2        MARK           [     2] [   C06C1412]  10-20-1989   4:15 pm
     3        PCBOARD        [   250] [         5F]  10-19-1989  11:21 am
     4        PAUL           [   255] [         9D]  10-20-1989   4:33 pm
     6        ERIC           [   250] [         6F]  10-20-1989  12:32 pm
     7        CARL           [   250] [         4D]  10-20-1989   8:18 am
     8      * MARK           [   250] [         98]  10-20-1989   3:56 pm
    15        PAUL           [     2] [   C0DB6714]  10-20-1989   3:32 pm
    16        LESLIE         [   250] [         3F]  10-20-1989   9:20 am

F:\PUBLIC)
```

Fig. B-6. An example of the USERLIST command.

time for each server and optionally your Group affiliation, your Security and your Rights. The applicable options are:

Option	Description
/G	Group Membership
/S	Security Equivalences
/R	Rights
/A	All information

The Novell Command Line Utilities provide a comprehensive suite of programs and utilities to accomplish wide ranging tasks in the network environment. Each release of the product carries with it new commands and/or enhancements which are designed to provide even greater functionality and ease of use.

THE NOVELL CONSOLE COMMANDS

There are a number of Novell commands and utilities that only work from the console. Other commands are provided that work from the console as a convenience. The console is the interactive command interpreter on the file server itself. The commands can be grouped as in the following sections.

FILE SERVER INFORMATION

MONITOR
MONITOR [station number]

This command displays the Novell Monitor screen with the now familiar Novell grid. The grid shows active station connections and the file activity, by station.

CLEAR STATION
CLEAR STATION n

This command will disconnect the indicated station from the network. There is no caution message or opportunity to back out, so use with caution.

CONFIG
CONFIG

The CONFIG command is used to display the configuration of the file server including types and addresses of the file servers network boards and the number of file server processes.

NAME
NAME

Displays the file server's name.

OFF
OFF

Clears the monitor and places a colon prompt in the upper left of the screen.

TRACK
TRACK ON/OFF

This is an undocumented console command that shows the inter server communications. Each file server advertises itself once a minute. The IN prefix indicates a message received by the server and an OUT prefix indicates a message sent. Normally used only in network diagnostics.

SENDING MESSAGES

BROADCAST
BROADCAST message

This command is used to send a message from the console to all attached workstations. It is used to alert users when the server is going to be down for maintenance, etc.

CLEAR MESSAGE
CLEAR MESSAGE

This command is used to clear messages from the message line on the console.

SEND
SEND message [TO] [STATION] [stationlist]

The console SEND command, like the command line utility SEND, is used to send short messages to selected workstations.

LOGGING INTO THE NETWORK

DISABLE/ENABLE LOGIN
DISABLE/ENABLE LOGIN

The Disable Login prevents users from logging into the network. The Enable Login allows users to log back into a network after the DISABLE command has been issued.

PRINTING

PRINTER

The printer command takes eight different forms. These forms are used to manage the printers attached to the file server on the network.

PRINTER *nn* FORM[MOUNT] *xx*   Notifies the server that the printer's paper has been changed.

PRINTER *nn* FORM FEED   Advances the paper one page in the specified printer.

PRINTERS Lists information about the printers that are attached to the file server.

PRINTER *xx* MARK [[TOP OF] FORM] Prints asterisks on the indicated printer to assist with aligning pre-printed forms.

PRINTER *nn* REWIND *xx* [PAGES] Rewinds the current spool the number of pages indicated and resumes printing at that point.

PRINTER *nn* START Restarts a printer that has been stopped with the STOP command.

PRINTER *nn* STOP Stops the printing on the specified printer.

NOTE: In the above commands the PRINTER command can be abbreviated to just the letter P, thus P 1 STOP is equivalent to PRINTER 1 STOP.

MANAGING PRINT QUEUES AND SPOOLERS

There are a variety of commands that can be used for management of the various print queues and spoolers. The form of these commands and their function is summarized here:

PRINTER *nn* ADD [QUEUE] *name* [[AT]] [PRIORITY]*xx* This command adds an existing queue to the specified printer for servicing.

QUEUE *name* CHANGE [JOB]*nn*[TO] [PRIORITY]*xx* This command changes the order of the specified job within its queue.

SPOOL *nn* [TO] [QUEUE] *name* Redirects NetWare 2.0 spool jobs to a NetWare 2.1 queue.

QUEUE *name* CREATE This command creates a new queue on the server with the name indicated.

QUEUE *name* DELETE [JOB] Deletes jobs currently present in the indicated queue.

PRINTER *nn* DELETE QUEUE *name* Removes a queue from the named printer's service.

QUEUE *name* DESTROY Destroys the specified queue.

QUEUES Lists the current queues on the file server.

SPOOL Displays the file server's current spool mappings.

QUEUE *name* [JOBS] Displays the jobs present in the printer's queue.

NOTE: In the above commands the key words PRINTER, QUEUE, and SPOOL can be abbreviated P, Q, and S, respectively.

OTHER CONSOLE COMMANDS

DISK Lists the status of all of the network drives in the server.

DOWN This command brings the server down in an orderly fashion. Clears all cache buffers, closes all files and shuts down the NOS process.

VAP Lists the current VAPS that have been added to the file server and are currently operating.

UNMIRROR/REMIRROR *nn* In SFT NetWare this command is used to shut down or restart the mirroring feature for the specified drive.

CONSOLE This command is used in Non-dedicated NetWare systems to move from a DOS process to the NetWare Console.

DOS This command is used in Non-dedicated NetWare systems to exit the Console process and move to DOS.

MOUNT [PACK] [*vol number*] Used in systems with removable disk packs to mount a volume.

DISMOUNT [PACK] [*vol number*] Used in systems with removable disk packs to dismount removable volumes.

Appendix C
TES Compatible Emulation Packages

TES supports any terminal emulation package that can support the INT 14 interface. Several companies provide this interface currently. Some of these do require a supplement driver to support INT 14. Currently supported terminal emulators for TES are:

- InterTerm (Interconnections, Inc.)
- Reflections (Walker Richer and Quinn)
- PCTERM (Crystal Point)
- Eicom (Softronics)
- Polystar 220 (polygon)
- ZStem (Persoft)
- Softerm PC (Softronics)
- EM220 (Diversified Computer Systems, Inc.)

Appendix D
Advanced Printing

One of the benefits of Novell's CompuServe NetWire forum is learning how people work with NetWare to achieve the greatest flexibility. One such work-around is the following patch to Novell's printing utilities to achieve greater management with printing.

GLOBAL PRINTCON

The following was put together so that each user does not have to have a defined PRINTCON.DAT file copied for them. It enables the supervisor to create a single PRINTCON.DAT file for all users to access. If you create a printcon default database, as outlined in Chapter 9, then you have to use the Supervisor—"Copy Print Job Configurations" option in PRINTCON for everybody's login name. It is strongly recommended that you keep an unmodified copy of the NetWare utilities and test any versions you modify completely before letting users work with them.

The following example is shown for the CAPTURE command but the same technique can be used on all NetWare printing utilities where they store their default files:

1. Rename CAPTURE.EXE to C, or something without an .EXE extension.

2. Type DEBUG C, as shown in Fig. D-1.

3. At the – prompt type: scs:100 ffff 'sys:mail'   It will return and display an address, like: 2770:858F

4. The number on the right side of the :, in this case, 858F, will be the offset that holds the location of the PRINTCON.DAT file directory. We will use this number to change the default directory for our global printcon.

5. Next type: f858F L1c 'sys:mail \ printcon.dat',0,0, 0,0,0,0,0 except use your address instead of the 858F address.

```
C:\>debug c.
-scs:100 ffff 'sys:mail'
25B7:858F
-d 858f
25B7:8580                                                    73                    s
25B7:8590   79 73 3A 6D 61 69 6C 5C-25 6C 78 5C 25 73 00 70   ys:mail\%lx\%s.p
25B7:85A0   72 69 6E 74 63 6F 6E 2E-64 61 74 00 00 53 59 53   rintcon.dat..SYS
25B7:85B0   3A 50 55 42 4C 49 43 5C-4E 45 54 24 50 52 4E 2E   :PUBLIC\NET$PRN.
25B7:85C0   44 41 54 00 00 00 00 00-CE 0A B2 20 20 00 B0 21   DAT........ ..!
25B7:85D0   22 23 24 25 26 27 28 29-2A 2B 2C 2D 2E 2F 30 31   "#$%&'()*+,-./01
25B7:85E0   32 33 34 35 36 37 38 39-3A 3B 3C 3D 3E 3F 40 41   23456789:;<=>?@A
25B7:85F0   42 43 44 45 46 47 48 49-4A 4B 4C 4D 4E 4F 50 51   BCDEFGHIJKLMNOPQ
25B7:8600   52 53 54 55 56 57 58 59-5A 5B 2F 5D 5E 20 60      RSTUVWXYZ[/]^ `
-f858f L1c 'sys:mail\printcon.dat',0,0,0,0,0,0,0
-d 858f
25B7:8580                                                    73                    s
25B7:8590   79 73 3A 6D 61 69 6C 5C-70 72 69 6E 74 63 6F 6E   ys:mail\printcon
25B7:85A0   2E 64 61 74 00 00 00 00-00 00 00 00 00 53 59 53   .dat.........SYS
25B7:85B0   3A 50 55 42 4C 49 43 5C-4E 45 54 24 50 52 4E 2E   :PUBLIC\NET$PRN.
25B7:85C0   44 41 54 00 00 00 00 00-CE 0A B2 20 20 00 B0 21   DAT........ ..!
25B7:85D0   22 23 24 25 26 27 28 29-2A 2B 2C 2D 2E 2F 30 31   "#$%&'()*+,-./01
25B7:85E0   32 33 34 35 36 37 38 39-3A 3B 3C 3D 3E 3F 40 41   23456789:;<=>?@A
25B7:85F0   42 43 44 45 46 47 48 49-4A 4B 4C 4D 4E 4F 50 51   BCDEFGHIJKLMNOPQ
25B7:8600   52 53 54 55 56 57 58 59-5A 5B 2F 5D 5E 20 60      RSTUVWXYZ[/]^ `
-
```

Fig. D-1. The screen displayed after typing DEBUG C:.

6. At the – prompt, type W and press the Enter key (the system will display Writing xxxx bytes).

7. Now, type q, for quit.

8. Rename C. to GCAPTURE.EXE.

Now put your "GLOBAL" PRINTCON in the SYS:MAIL directory. If you have one made up it should be in the supervisor's mail directory, which is the SYS:MAIL ＼ 1 directory. The same patch works with NPRINT (just patch all addresses you find that are applicable—there are more than one in a few of the utilities.) You can also point the path of the PRINTCON default database to use the printcon.dat that resides in the SUPERVISOR(user)'s mailbox directory, which is always SYS:MAIL ＼ 1.

Index